Douglas

HISTORIC COMMERCIAL AIRCRAFT SERIES, VOLUME 13

Contents page image: (Photo courtesy of Eddie Coates Collection)

Published by Key Books
An imprint of Key Publishing Ltd
PO Box 100
Stamford
Lincs PE9 1XQ

ISBN 978 1 80282 370 7

www.keypublishing.com

Original edition published as *Aeroplane Classic Airliner: The Douglas DC-3* © 2014, edited by Tim McLelland

This edition © 2022

Typeset by SJmagic DESIGN SERVICES, India.

Contents

Introduction

Commercial aircraft are a fundamental part of modern society, contributing to communications and commerce across the globe. It would be difficult to underestimate their importance when one considers the many ways in which they have enabled nations to flourish and grow, and how they have truly made the world a much smaller place. The origins of commercial aviation can, of course, be traced right back to the very earliest days of powered flight, but the development of what is now known as the ubiquitous "airliner" is a slightly shorter story. Although many early aircraft were designed to carry passengers, the creation of a truly practical and versatile airliner is a story that began with American designer Donald Douglas, and the legendary DC-3. It is fair to say that the DC-3 was the very first true airliner, and it paved the way for the hundreds of increasingly advanced commercial aircraft that have emerged over the 80 years since Douglas' design was developed. It is important to consider that the DC-3 was not a one-off design created from scratch. It was in fact a development of the DC-1 and DC-2, two aircraft that incorporated some significant differences to the DC-3 that succeeded them, but which were in effect the same design. Because these designs emerged shortly before the outbreak of World War Two, it was inevitable that military applications for the aircraft would influence its development, and the sudden need for a versatile and capable transport

aircraft led to the creation of the C-47 – a military derivative of the DC-3, designed to cater for the requirements of the military. The story of the C-47 is well known, but the history of the civil DC-3 (which directly led to the creation of the C-47) is often overlooked, having been overshadowed by the exploits of its military counterpart. This is perhaps understandable, but it would be wrong to underestimate the importance of the DC-3, not only because it was in effect the very same aircraft as the C-47, but also because it was the first (and therefore the most significant) airliner ever built. It is ironic that after World War Two ended, countless examples of the military C-47 were suddenly declared redundant, and they were resold to civilian buyers around the world, their abundance (and inexpensiveness) enabling many fledgling airlines and other commercial operators to grow and prosper. These former military C-47s soon became the most familiar and ubiquitous derivative of the DC-3, and, despite their origins, the C-47 and DC-3 inevitably became one and the same, with only logbooks and a few physical variations (most notably the C-47's larger cargo door) distinguishing one from the other. Perhaps the most remarkable aspect of the DC-3's story is that the aircraft is still very much in business today. Even though the aircraft has long since made way for larger, faster and more capable airliners, the DC-3 is still a sturdy, versatile, inexpensive and reliable aircraft. Countless commercial operators around the world continue to use the aircraft for cargo hauling, passenger flying and many other specialized tasks. Because the DC-3 is a simple and rugged aircraft, it can be repaired cheaply and refurbished whenever necessary, bestowing an almost infinite life span on its aged airframe. Although the numbers of active aircraft inevitably dwindle with time, it would be impossible to predict when the very last examples will finally be withdrawn from commercial use. The mighty DC-3 will seemingly fly forever.

Chapter 1

Early Days

The young Donald Douglas grew up on the streets of Brooklyn, New York, sharing his childhood between the city and his parents' property on Long Island, where he enjoyed swimming and sailing. When he was not relaxing, he spent much of his time studying. Douglas became a passionate sailor, but he grew to share his passion with a completely different mode of transport – the aeroplane. William Douglas (Donald's father) encouraged his son's studies by making a trip to the Smithsonian Institution's National Museum in Washington, and it was during this seminal visit that Donald first saw the "Langley Experimental Airplane Engine" on display. The contraption fascinated him, and the engine's accompanying notes described the thrilling concepts of flying machines. Douglas was only 11 years old when the Wright Brothers completed their historic first flight at Kitty Hawk, and although the notion of achieving powered flight was still a great novelty, Douglas resolved to learn more about the world of aviation, and in 1904, when he was just 12, he read a detailed account of the Wright Brothers' flight in *The Aeronautical Journal*, and four years later he delighted in watching the Wright Brothers demonstrate their flying capabilities at Curtiss Field on Long Island, where their flimsy flying machine was shown to invited guests, before being unveiled to the general public. Douglas later claimed that although his early visit to the Smithsonian Institution had sparked his initial enthusiasm, it was this flying demonstration on Long Island that truly marked the beginning of his long and distinguished career in aviation. After graduation, he enrolled at the US Naval Academy at Annapolis, where he devoted much of his spare time to building model aircraft, some of which he hung from his dormitory ceiling. If he was not building models, he could inevitably be found drawing aircraft designs, and it was not surprising that he petitioned the Academy to devise a course in Aeronautical studies. But at that time, the Academy had no interest in the subject and in 1912 Douglas left Annapolis, after having learned of a new aeronautical curriculum being introduced at the Massachusetts Institute of Technology (MIT). His time at Annapolis had equipped him with a great deal of knowledge and many useful contacts within the US Navy, but he took his Bachelor of Science Degree to Massachusetts and joined the first aeronautical class at MIT. After graduating, he stayed at MIT for another year as an Assistant Instructor in aeronautical engineering, after which he joined the Connecticut Aircraft Company as a design engineer, working on the US Navy's first dirigible.

Douglas applied to join the Glenn L. Martin Company during 1915 and after reading his references and credentials from MIT and Annapolis, Martin immediately invited Douglas to their headquarters in Los Angeles and offered Douglas a position in the company. It was not long before he had designed the Martin Model S, a machine that held a world endurance and altitude record for some time. His time with

Donald Wills Douglas, born April 6, 1892, founder of the Douglas Aircraft Company. Douglas died on February 1, 1981. (Tim McLelland collection)

Martin was both rewarding and enjoyable but by 1916 Douglas had decided to leave the company so that he could contribute to the country's war effort. He moved to Washington as Chief Civilian Aeronautical Engineer for the US Army Signal Corps and became established as one of the world's first aircraft engineers, equipped not with qualifications but a wealth of experience and knowledge. He later commented that: "it was all done by judgment in those days. If the airplane flew the judgment was good. If it didn't, the judgment was bad." But, despite his value as a talented design engineer, Douglas could not cope with the military's stifling bureaucracy, and he soon found himself returning to his position with Martin in Los Angeles, where he worked on the creation of the Martin MB-1 bomber. This large, twin-engine aircraft effectively began the development of the United States' strategic air power capability, and it remained in service with the US Navy and Marines for more than a decade. Douglas was immensely satisfied with the MB-1's capabilities, and he wisely considered that the same aircraft might also be suitable for more peaceful uses as a civilian carrier of passengers or cargo, even though few others shared the same belief.

He stated that:

> Speed is the most outstanding present-day advantage of the airplane. I rank passenger carrying first in importance. Correspondence or the telephone cannot supply the complete satisfaction of actual personal contact. Where any great distance separates the subject and his objective, present-day express train service often proves too slow. Commercial operators must take the risk. One way or another they must carry passengers on schedule, comfortably, and without a mishap for a reasonable period.

He added that, "where speed is of the quintessence of transportation, the airplane will have a definite field and a profitable one." His words were prophetic, but in the United States there was little enthusiasm to share his vision, even though developments on the other side of the Atlantic were progressing with some speed.

Designed by the Davis-Douglas Company, the Cloudster was designed to make a non-stop flight across the continental USA. The coast-to-coast flight attempt was thwarted by engine failure, and the abandoned attempt prompted Davis to leave the company, thereby creating the new Douglas Company. (Tim McLelland collection)

The Douglas World Cruiser was designed in response to a US Army Air Service requirement for an aircraft capable of flying around the world. Two aircraft completed their world tour in 1924. The Cruiser's success and notoriety established Douglas as a leading designer and manufacturer. (Tim McLelland collection)

The Fokker Tri-Motor (together with a similar design created by Ford) became popular with emerging airlines during the late 1920s. The crash of TWA's Fokker F.10 in 1931 – caused by poor maintenance and its plywood construction – led to the introduction of safer and more robust aircraft, particularly all-metal aircraft such as the Douglas DC-2. (Tim McLelland collection)

Clover Field (pictured in 1929) was named after World War One pilot Greayer Clover. It became the home of the Douglas Aircraft Company and eventually developed into what is now Santa Monica Municipal Airport. The large Douglas Company hangars are visible on the airfield perimeter. (Tim McLelland collection)

DC-1 X223Y, pictured at Clover Field shortly before the aircraft made its first flight on July 1, 1933. Remarkably, despite the significance of this event, no official photographs of the maiden flight were taken. (Tim McLelland collection)

Above: X223Y pictured during preparations for its maiden flight in 1933. Just visible on the tail is the Douglas Company's "First Around the World" logo and motto, and the temporarily applied "X" serial prefix. (Tim McLelland collection)

Left: This rare image shows X223Y in flight over California. Following the maiden flight, full registration titles were applied to the upper starboard wing, together with TWA's company letters on the port wing. (Tim McLelland collection)

Below: One of the very first photographs ever taken of DC-1 X223Y, shortly after rollout at Clover Field. As can be seen, the airframe was remarkably simple and streamlined compared to contemporary commercial designs.

After entering commercial service, X223Y became NC223Y and (as can just be seen on the nose) was named *City of Los Angeles*. By this stage, the tail and rudder assembly had been redesigned, following early stability problems. (Tim McLelland collection)

Pictured in front of the vintage air terminal buildings at Glendale, NC223Y features company number "300" on the tail. Also visible is the tail wheel aerodynamic fairing that was soon removed, having proved to be of little value. (Tim McLelland collection)

Chapter 2

Between the Wars

The end of World War One resulted in a drastic reduction in aircraft production capacity within the United States. In just six months, no less than 21 major aviation companies closed down, and with surplus military aircraft scattered across the country, the aircraft industry struggled to survive. Douglas was by now Martin's chief engineer and so his position was secure, even though the company's future was uncertain. Its MB-1 looked set to achieve good sales figures thanks to its performance and capabilities, but with no clear requirement for significant numbers of new military aircraft, the future seemed bleak. However, Douglas still believed in the value of commercial aviation, even though there was scarcely any sign of such potential in 1918. There was a rather unreliable Post Office air mail service that relied on flimsy de Havilland DH.4s and a flying boat service that operated to and from Catalina Island, but there was very little else. Martin had no interest in anything other than military aircraft, and so Douglas decided to take a bold step and resign from Martin, taking his US$600 savings, wife and two children to Santa Monica in order to establish his very own company. Situated to

Newark Airport, February 1949, and NC223Y is pictured after having completed a record-breaking flight from California. As can be seen, media interest in the new DC-1 reached almost hysterical proportions, leading to swift and substantial commercial success for Douglas. (Tim McLelland collection)

the rear of a barber's shop, he set-up his fledgling business in a tiny 18sq ft room, equipped with little more than a desk and telephone. He desperately needed finance, and he immediately embarked on a search for businessmen who could support his plans to design and develop commercial aircraft. With his impressive background and letters of recommendation from many influential people, Douglas was well placed to secure the serious interest of any would-be investor, but nobody believed that there was any practical future in commercial aviation. It was the chance meeting with old friend Bill Henry that changed Douglas' fortunes. Henry was a sportswriter for the *Los Angeles Times,* and he was following the story of wealthy sportsman David Davis, who wanted to fly non-stop across the continental USA – a feat that had yet to be achieved. Henry telephoned the sportsman and with some delight he then informed Douglas that money would be made available to him, if he could design and manufacture an aircraft capable of making a cross-country flight. Douglas was not entirely enthusiastic, as he had anticipated the design of numerous aircraft rather than just one, but Henry assured him that if he took on this record-breaking project, the ensuing publicity would doubtless give him all the finances he needed. In July 1920, Douglas met Davis and an agreement was made to create a unique racing place for the project, with a sum of US$40,000 under the control of what would now be the Davis-Douglas Company.

After sending invitations to some of his former colleagues at Martin, a group of five men duly resigned from their positions at Martin to join the new Davis-Douglas Company in California. They were astonished to find that they were now assigned to a tiny office behind a barber's shop, but they knew that Douglas had the ability to build not only the one-off racing plane but many more significant subsequent designs, and they were sufficiently confident to take a gamble and abandon their well-paid jobs with Martin. Their confidence was well-placed, and most of this small team remained together

Static tests on the DC-1's wing loading capability were performed in a surprisingly improvised manner, using manually loaded weights and calibration devices placed on the hangar floor. (Tim McLelland collection)

for decades, as part of what eventually became the world's most famous aircraft manufacturer. They designed and built the new Cloudster machine on the second floor of a timber mill, where space restrictions required the team to manufacture the aircraft in sections that could be lowered out of the upper floor window and then assembled for flight at the Goodyear Airfield in East Los Angeles. The Cloudster made its first flight on February 24, 1921, and achieved a very respectable 85mph top speed together with a new altitude record of 19,160ft. The record cross-country attempt began on June 21, but a mechanical failure forced Davis to land in Texas and while repairs were being made, a vicious storm blew the Cloudster upside-down, causing significant damage. By the time the aircraft had been returned to California and rebuilt, a US Army T-2 had claimed the cross-country record, and the hapless Cloudster lost its chance to enter the record books. But it had earned Douglas a great deal of national media coverage, even though Davis was left with only a shattered dream and an empty bank balance. He sold his share of the company to Douglas for US$2,500, and in 1921, the small team re-emerged as the Douglas Company, before becoming the Douglas Aircraft Company in 1928. By this stage, the US government was becoming increasingly eager to develop military aviation in many forms, and Douglas (in an ironic reversal of his attitude whilst working for Martin) considered the possibility of developing the Cloudster into a military machine. He lobbied officials in Washington and secured an agreement to develop the aircraft into a torpedo bomber. Harry Chandler (owner of the *Los Angeles Times*) secured the interest of some wealthy colleagues, and they put some US$1,500 into the company so that manufacture of the military Cloudster (the DT-1) could begin. An initial three DT-1 prototype aircraft were followed by a larger order for DT-2 aircraft, and, at long last, Douglas was manufacturing airplanes.

Development of new designs immediately followed, although the gradual emergence of serious interest in commercial aviation was not without its problems for Douglas. Passenger flying was still comparatively uncommon by 1928, and although some air taxi services were operating around the US, most commercial flying was still devoted to mail and cargo services. Even so, some 16 fatal crashes occurred in that year, and the situation grew worse a year later. Enthusiasm for civilian flying began

DC-2s pictured as they near completion at Santa Monica. Douglas employed a production-line system for the new airliner, paving the way for modern commercial aircraft manufacturing techniques. (Tim McLelland collection)

to wane. Recently, Douglas had enjoyed a period of great success and fame following the creation of their World Cruiser aircraft in response to an Army project to complete an historic round-the-world flight. These aircraft completed their world tour in 1924, and the event led to an order for military versions of the aircraft in the shape of the "XO" model. The development of mail services had also created significant work for Douglas, and some 59 aircraft were manufactured specifically for this purpose. Douglas later said: "these early structures, designed expressly to carry the mail, were the foundations for the DC airliners that were to come." He also said that he "built mail planes because I couldn't sell people on the dream I had from the beginning, large commercial transports. I knew the day was coming when everybody would want to travel by air, but I had to wait." But with a seemingly endless number of accidents and fatal crashes appearing in the media, Douglas had an uphill task in persuading the country's fledgling airlines to buy any form of passenger transport aircraft. Douglas created the C-1, a small six-passenger aircraft, but no serious commercial interest in the aircraft was forthcoming, and eventually only 26 aircraft were sold to the US Army, as its very first cargo aircraft. Rather more successful was the Dolphin, a small twin-engine amphibian that attracted modest but steady sales. It was primarily this design that helped the Douglas Company to prosper, and by the time that the company became re-established at a new and much larger factory site at Clover Field, some 200 engineers were working for Douglas and the company was already grossing some US$2m annually. Passenger flying was still in its earliest days, but Douglas believed that despite the setbacks, interest would grow. His confidence proved to be well-founded, and by 1930, a staggering 383 different aircraft types were carrying passengers around the US, courtesy of the manufacturing facilities of no less than 80 different companies. It was clear by now that bigger and better commercial passenger transport aircraft would continue to emerge, and Douglas might finally get his opportunity to create the aircraft that he'd dreamed of for so long.

An interesting nose-on view of a DC-2, as delivered to American Airlines. This viewpoint illustrates the slimmer proportions of the DC-2's fuselage compared to the DC-3. (Tim McLelland collection)

Boeing 247D NR257Y earned the dubious distinction of coming third in the 1934 London to Melbourne Air Race, with a time that was almost three hours behind the Douglas DC-2. The race secured the success of the DC-2 and sealed the fate of the inferior Boeing aircraft. (Tim McLelland collection)

Early TWA DC-2s were fitted with aerodynamic fairings over the fixed tail wheel and small doors that closed over the retracted main wheels. These were soon found to be of little value, and they were deleted from production. (Tim McLelland collection)

DC-2 PH-AKO was part of KLM's fleet until May 10, 1940, when the Luftwaffe's Kampfgeschwader 4 bombed Amsterdam's Schipol Airport, destroying several aircraft, including this example. (Tim McLelland)

Pictured during 1939, a KLM DC-3 shares ramp space with a DC-2 from Polish airline LOT at Lydda Airport. (Tim McLelland collection)

Swissair acquired its DC-2 fleet during 1934, some six aircraft being manufactured under license by Fokker. They were retired in 1952. (R. A. Scholefield collection)

DC-2 EC-EBB joined Spanish airline LAPE in 1936, named *Sagitario*. It subsequently joined Iberia as EC-AGN and finally EC-AAB (renamed as *Ramon Franco*) before being withdrawn in 1947. (Eddie Coates collection)

Polish Airlines purchased three DC-2 aircraft. SP-ASJ survived only until November 1937, when it crashed in Bulgaria. SP-ASK was interned in Riga during 1939 while SP-ASL (illustrated at Lydda) was similarly interned in Romania shortly after these photographs were taken. (Eddie Coates collection)

Chapter 3

An Airliner at Last

Transcontinental and Western Air (TWA) acquired a fleet of 19 Ford Trimotor aircraft, and in 1932 the company established a regular passenger and mail service between New York and Los Angeles, replacing older Fokker Trimotor aircraft that had been assigned to this route for some time. The Fokker aircraft had first been introduced because of their superior load carrying capability when compared to the Douglas aircraft that had been used previously. However, on March 31, 1931, one of TWA's Fokker aircraft crashed in Kansas while flying through a storm. Investigations revealed that the aircraft's wing had failed while battling turbulence. Crucially, no proper inspection procedures had been in place for the aircraft, and the wooden structure had simply rotted away.

Safer and more reliable aircraft were desperately needed, and with the Fokker aircraft grounded, TWA assigned Ford Trimotors to the long cross-country route between Los Angeles and New York. But by the end of 1932, TWA's Ford aircraft were almost as exhausted as its troubled Fokker fleet, and the airline looked for a new aircraft. Fortunately for TWA, a very suitable aircraft was available in the shape of the Boeing 247. This aircraft had been developed by Boeing after a failed attempt to secure a military order for a new bomber design.

Surprisingly, very few photographs were taken of DC-3 production. This rare image shows DC-3 airframes awaiting assembly at the Douglas Santa Monica factory.

The very first Douglas Sleeper Transport (DST) (DC-3) was NC14988, which joined American Airlines in 1936. It was sold to TWA in March 1942 but by the end of that month it had been assigned to the USAAF as a C-49E (42-43619). It survived only a few weeks before being written-off in an accident at Knobnoster, Missouri, on October 15, 1942. (R. A. Scholefield collection)

Boeing's XB-9 looked set to be purchased for the US Army, but Douglas' old friends at the Martin Company produced a better design, and the Boeing bomber was therefore redundant. Boeing resolved to develop the aircraft into a commercial transport aircraft and for TWA the fast, all-metal stressed skin Boeing 247 looked like an ideal replacement for their weary Ford and Fokker fleet. It was a very impressive design with outstanding performance and features that would enable passengers to fly in levels of comfort that had hitherto been unheard of.

TWA's Jack Frye went to Boeing and immediately placed an order for the 247, and Boeing eagerly accepted the order, but only on the basis that an order for 60 aircraft for United Airlines would have to be completed first. For Boeing, the United Airlines order was a hugely significant one that required all the resources of their early manufacturing facility in Seattle, and it soon became clear that fulfilling orders for any additional customers would not be possible for at least two years. TWA soon accepted that Boeing would not increase its manufacturing capacity and that a two-year wait would be necessary if the airline was to obtain the 247. But TWA was struggling with decreasing revenues, and it seemed certain that if no new fleet was acquired soon, the company might fold. As an alternative, TWA decided to approach Douglas.

On August 2, 1932, Donald Douglas received a letter from Jack Frye, Vice President of TWA. Douglas later described this communication as "the birth certificate of the DC ships." Frye outlined TWA's requirement for at least ten new aircraft, which would be powered by three engines, possess a range of 1,000 miles and have a top speed of 185mph. Frye stipulated that the new aircraft would have to be capable of carrying at least 12 passengers and two crew, and also asked how long the Douglas Aircraft Company would need to develop such an aircraft, as time was an important factor. Donald Douglas examined the letter with a mixture of emotions. The potential order appealed to his long-stifled ambition to create a significant new passenger aircraft, but his company had survived and eventually prospered on a series of orders from the military, and diverting company resources to a major commercial design would be a risky move.

This excellent photograph of NC14988 clearly illustrates the upper cabin windows that were common to early DST aircraft. Photographs suggest that the precise number of upper windows varied, depending on customer requirements. (*Aeroplane* collection)

He called in his Assistant Chief Engineer Arthur Raymond, Executive Vice President James "Dutch" Kindelberger, and General Manager Harry Wetzel.

Raymond recalled:

> [I] felt a sense of urgency in the air. I remember watching Doug study a piece of paper in front of him. Without a word he looked up, and passed the paper to me. I read Frye's letter and Doug asked me if we could build an airplane to the specifications in the letter. There isn't a plane in the world that can do all this, I told him. I wasn't sure that the specifications were realistic.

The assembled group eventually agreed, however, that although the United States economy was in a terrible state, it was probably the right time to take the company into the commercial transport business and a plan was made to create some initial design studies during the following week. Raymond's initial caution was not without foundation, and from the outset he dismissed the requirement for three engines: "Right from the start we ruled out a tri-motor and considered a bi-motor, meeting the engine-out requirement. The ability to fly with one engine dead was a very important consideration in commercial aviation in those days." Raymond and his colleagues worked hard over the following few days to create a proposal that would meet TWA's requirements, and a week later, the design team boarded a train for the long journey to New York. Raymond used the trip to devote his time to detailed calculations so that when the team arrived at TWA's office on Lexington Avenue, they were well equipped with a very thorough and detailed proposal.

When the team finally laid out their proposals and drawings before Frye and TWA's President Richard Robbins, there was no sense of excitement. Robbins immediately called in technical advisor Charles Lindbergh, who studied the specifications and said, "If an engine should fail on take off, we want to be able to climb out with a full load on the remaining engine. If you're going to build a bi-motor as your drawings suggest, we still want the engine-out requirement. We want to be able to climb to an altitude of 8,000 feet, the highest point on our route system, and maintain level flight on the one engine." Fry asked, "Can you do it?" Raymond was not sure, and he reached for a pencil and slide ruler, frantically making calculations on the edges of the drawing that was laid on the desk before them. The room remained quiet, and it was Lindbergh who broke the silence, saying: "If you can do it we'll buy the design. If not, we'll go elsewhere." Raymond effectively had the future of the Douglas Aircraft Company in his hands. He could not risk leaving New York without an order, and so he replied that he could indeed meet the requirement, even though he was far from certain that the requirement was a realistic one.

Raymond telephoned Donald Douglas to give him the encouraging news, and it was not surprising that "Doug" (as he was referred to by everyone in the company) was delighted, even though Raymond admitted that it was he who was "the one with the butterflies." Despite his worries, Raymond based his assertions on experience he had gleaned from a four-year course at California Institute of Technology, where he had lectured on aircraft design. During his stay there, he had tasked one of his students (W. Bailey Oswald, better known as "Ozzy") with the creation of a performance calculation system, based on the use of a slide rule, covering variables such as atmospheric density, airframe drag, engine output and propeller efficiency.

Peering through KLM's circular hangar windows, a pair of DC-2s can be seen sharing hangar space with six DC-3s during November 1939. The huge neutrality markings on the aircraft fuselages were also applied to the upper wings of some aircraft, as can be seen here. (*Aeroplane* collection)

Lufthansa purchased DC-2 D-ABEQ *Taunus* from Fokker in 1935. Lufthansa sold it in 1937, but later operated ten captured examples during World War Two. (*Aeroplane* collection)

This system formed the basis of Raymond's calculations, as he later recalled: "Using Ozzy's method, I concluded that a properly designed bi-motor, using the latest state-of-the-art technology, could probably do the job. The advantages of eliminating the nose engine were obvious, a clear front view for the crew, less noise and vibration, and no fumes in the cockpit."

Oswald himself recalled the following:

Raymond knew how to use my equations, and found that we could meet TWA's specifications with a two-engine airplane by shaping it properly. From the calculations we also decided that a stressed skin, all metal construction with brazen head rivets and wing flaps was a good way to build it.

No one could have taken such positive and decisive action as an assistant chief engineer for the layout as Mr. Raymond did. To my knowledge it had never been done before or afterward.

Certainly, Oswald's calculations indicated that a suitable aircraft could be produced, but with a 90 percent level of accuracy, there was always the worry that the ten percent risk of flawed calculations might prove to be Raymond's downfall, and he later admitted that he "had no idea what we were getting into when we began designing the DC-1."

TWA's Jack Frye later asked Raymond to go to the company's facility in Kansas City to look at more detailed specifications. Harry Wetzel returned to Los Angeles by train, but Raymond opted to fly to Kansas City, chiefly because he wanted an opportunity to gain his own experience of what it was like to fly on a TWA commercial flight in the Ford Tri-Motor. He believed that if he knew more about TWA's current standards, he'd be better placed to create something far better.

DC-2 1329, registered as A-500, was sold to Austria as a VIP transport for President Dollfuss during September 1934. It was sold to Swissair in April 1936 and reregistered HB-ISA. (Eddie Coates collection)

The long and bumpy flight at low altitude was enough to illustrate why most people preferred to travel by train. Equipped with the standard passenger issue of cotton wool ear plugs, a cup for air sickness and a bottle of smelling salts in case he felt faint, the flight was often uncomfortable and cold for Raymond, and it ended with a spray of muddy water from the aircraft's fresh air ventilators when the Tri-Motor finally touched down in the dark and rain. After recovering from the day-long flight, Raymond spent ten days with TWA's engineers, and he eventually returned to Los Angeles with more details of the kind of aircraft that TWA would really want.

From an engineering perspective, he wrote that the new aircraft should incorporate some key features that would drastically improve maintainability and reliability:

> It shall be possible to remove and replace complete landing gear and shock units by one man in one hour. The fuel system lines shall be completely removed by one man in 15 minutes. Each fuel tank shall be independently removed by two men in 30 minutes. The complete instrument panel shall be removable by one man in 25 minutes, exclusive of autopilot. Each surface control, ailerons, elevators and flaps shall be replaceable by two men in ten minutes.

Just as importantly, Raymond understood that the comfort of passengers was of paramount importance for a commercial operator and that "people should not be treated as cargo." Donald Douglas shared the same view, possibly as a result of his own experience of flying in the Ford Tri-motor. The new aircraft would require many new features that had nothing to do with aerodynamics but plenty to do with creature comforts. New levels of soundproofing would be introduced, better internal temperature control and insulation, better toilet facilities and more comfortable (and safer) seating too.

The design of the airframe relied quite significantly on work that had been done by Jack Northrop. He joined Douglas in 1923 and soon became an important figure in the design of the Douglas World Cruisers. He stayed with Douglas for only four years before joining Lockheed but when he left to form his own organization, Douglas became a 51 percent stockholder in the new Northrop Company. Jack Northrop developed the concept of monocoque production using both wood and metal. In this process, the outer covering absorbs much of the aircraft's structural strength.

He also developed a revolutionary wing structure based on European designs that incorporated a cantilever arrangement and several non-parallel aluminum spars that created a honeycomb effect,

With the crew in place, passengers board American Airlines *Flagship Texas* for an overnight flight to New York from Grand Central Air Terminal at Glendale, Los Angeles, late in 1937. A-115 is regarded as the "first DC-3," although the upper cabin windows illustrate that the aircraft was a DST. (Tim McLelland collection)

the multi-cellular arrangement creating structural strength that was much greater than that of the individual parts. These features became a fundamental part of the new Douglas design and contrasted with the features that had been incorporated into Boeing's more conventional 247. In that aircraft, the wing was manufactured in traditional fashion with two main truss beams that bisected the fuselage. The Douglas design had a flat center section to which removable outer panels could be attached. The fuselage simply rested on top of the flat center section, enabling a capacious and uninterrupted passenger and cargo cabin to be designed. The National Advisory Committee for Aeronautics (NACA – the forerunner of today's NASA) provided a great deal of assistance in designing the new wing, providing wind tunnel facilities in which a variety of wing sections of different thicknesses could be tested, the most suitable being selected for further development. It was accepted that tensional rigidity was important to avoid wing flutter at high speed, and so wing flex deflection was kept to an absolute minimum. The result was a wing structure that was immensely strong and one that reduced the overall weight of the aircraft. NACA also recommended a revised design for the aircraft's engine cowlings, and this reduced airframe drag, kept the engines cooler and helped to reduce internal cabin noise. Douglas decided to build a mechanical retraction gear for the aircraft's main wheels, after having learned of numerous failures in Boeing's 247 electrical system. The landing gear was therefore designed to use hydraulic power, retracting into the engine nacelles through the use of a long handle. The wheels retracted into a semi-recessed position that reduced airframe drag, but this still ensured that the tires stood proud of the nacelles so that in the event of a wheels-up forced landing, the wheels would still help to cushion the landing. When combined with the low-set wing, this would create a much better safety capability when compared to the older high-wing Tri-Motors and their fixed undercarriage.

A striking image that illustrates a huge leap in commercial air transport design. The first production DC-3, NC16001 *Flagship New York*, sits before the mighty *Hindenburg*. (Tim McLelland collection)

A classic promotional image showing the luxurious interior of the new DST, as a TWA flight attendant assists a mother and child, tucked-up in their sleeper berth. (Tim McLelland collection)

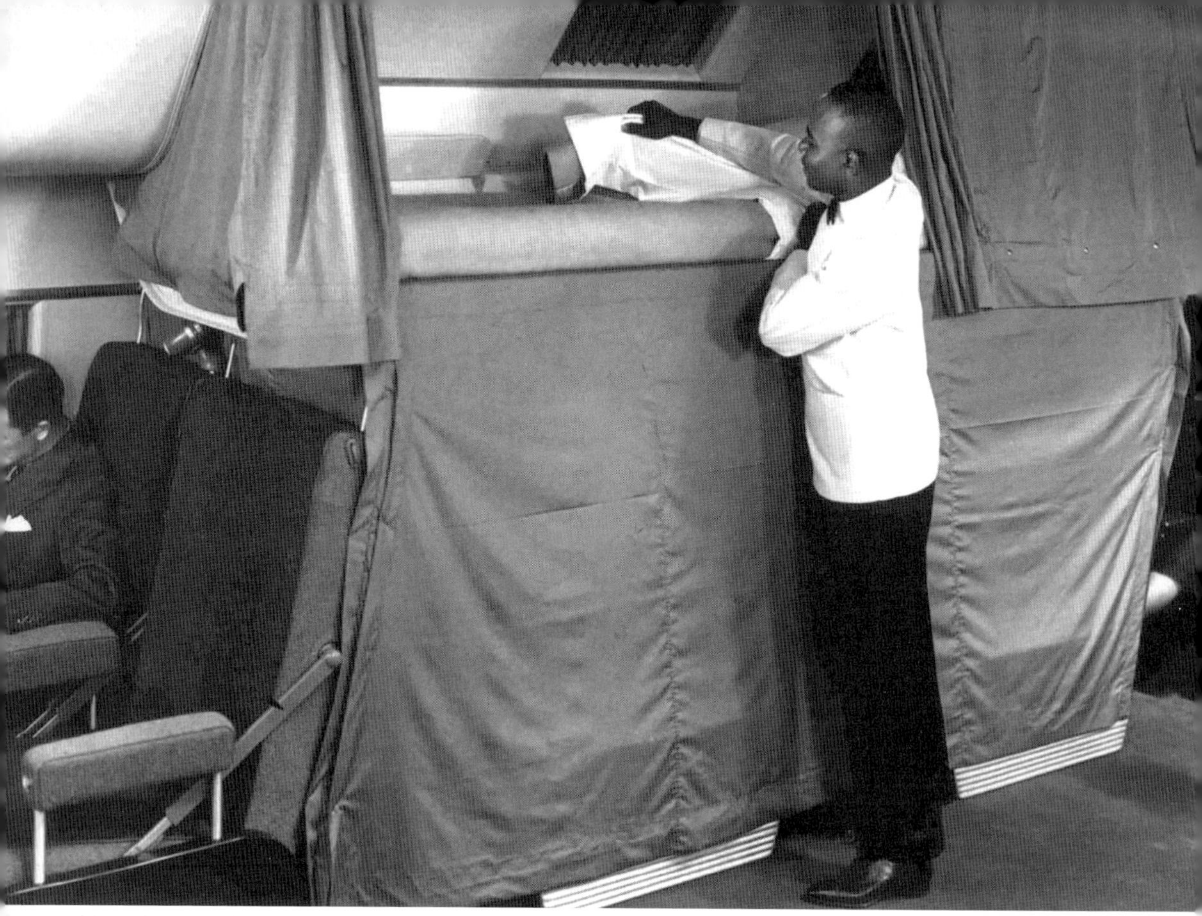

This early promotional photo shows part of the DST's internal layout, including the small upper windows fitted above the sleeper berths. The distance between the camera position and the steward suggests that this may have been a mock-up cabin. (Tim McLelland collection)

American Airlines NC17331 *Flagship Arkansas* is pictured as passengers board for a cross-country flight during 1939. (Tim McLelland collection)

High above the clouds, American Airlines NC28325 *Flagship San Francisco* illustrates the row of sleeper berth windows fitted to early DST DC-3s. It was later renamed *Flagship Monterrey*. (Tim McLelland collection)

TWA NC17312 *Luxury Sky Sleeper* pictured in flight during 1937. A partial fit of sleeping berth windows can be seen, in the forward cabin. (*Aeroplane* collection)

Chapter 4
Testing Times

TWA's Richard Robbins signed a contract with Douglas on September 20, 1932, for a sum of US$58,000, minus the cost of the engines. Douglas anticipated that it would cost as much as twice this figure to manufacture a prototype, but orders for production aircraft would recover this investment and TWA was offered an option to buy all or part of an initial 60-aircraft production run. Design of the aircraft began in earnest, with much of the early development taking place in NACA's wind tunnel facilities. Raymond's initial design calculations had allowed for a ten percent potential error, and the tunnel tests soon revealed that the mathematical equations did indeed need modification, just as Raymond had feared. Initial tests revealed a degree of instability, and it was only after a repositioned center-of-gravity position was examined, together with a revised wing sweep-back, that a satisfactory arrangement was found. Other significant design features were also established through the use of wind tunnel testing, not least the introduction of a fillet between the wing and fuselage, that promised to increase the aircraft's top speed by 17mph. Other small modifications improved predicted speed still further, including the substitution of a trailing radio antenna instead of a more conventional mast, and a fairing over the fixed tail wheel undercarriage, although this latter

The 13th DC-3 to be constructed, NC16013, joined American Airlines in September 1936, becoming *Flagship Virginia* until May 1939, when the aircraft was withdrawn. It eventually re-emerged as XA-HOT in Mexico. (R. A. Scholefield collection)

feature produced only a modest speed improvement and it was subsequently removed, chiefly because it added to maintenance requirements. Doors were also designed to cover the retracted main wheels, but these too produced only a negligible improvement in speed, and Douglas opted to abandon them in the interests of simplicity. Just as important was an indication that positioning the engine nacelles ahead of the wing leading edge would improve performance, as this would enable the landing gear to be positioned well ahead of the aircraft's center-of-gravity, thereby bestowing excellent ground stability on the aircraft. Oswald recalls that relying on wind tunnel testing was not without its risks in much the same way that mathematical calculations were also not entirely reliable.

We learned later to use caution in depending fully on wind tunnel tests. Often the results needed verification. We tried different things and many didn't work. We found it was very important to get a thorough dynamic test of the machine also. We had some ideas on how to improve lateral control, the yaw of the aeroplane, so we put a vane on top of the wing. In the wind tunnel it looked beautiful and it went through a stall very well. We then put it on the Northrop Gamma and Eddie Allen took it out and flew it. He went to roll it and it flipped over on its back. Naturally, we scrapped the idea.

The next step was to construct a full-scale mock-up of the aircraft, comprising of wooden frames covered with heavy paper to simulate the metal skin covering. This was the first time that any company had attempted to build a complete mock-up, and the result was a precise replication of the aircraft's components both in terms of dimensions and location within the airframe. Raymond recalled that the

Delta Airlines received its first DC-3s in 1940, eventually acquiring a fleet of around 25 aircraft. NC28340 *City of Atlanta* was delivered to Delta in November 1940, remaining in use until April 1953, when it was sold to Mohawk. (R. A. Scholefield collection)

aircraft's seats were designed to flip over in much the same way as contemporary tramcar seats had become commonplace. Built out of tubular metal, they were sturdy but far from attractive and less than comfortable. Even the upholstery was rather basic, in a dull brown color that reflected the designer's eye for practicality and function, rather than aesthetic appeal. Wall coverings and carpets of varying styles and colors were tried, but as Raymond admitted, they "didn't know very much in those days" and "attempts at color coordination looked like a psychedelic nightmare." But the seats were arranged with a generous 40 inches back-to-back separation and positioned so that they were all opposite a window and next to a wide, unobstructed aisle. Because the cabin was neatly positioned above the wing there was no internal wing spar obstruction and the windows could be fixed in a relatively high position, which provided the passengers with much improved vision and the spacious cabin enabled even the tallest person to walk through without stooping. A great deal of effort was devoted to the design of the flight deck, and both TWA and Douglas engineers spent endless days inside the cockpit, looking at ways in which the instrument layout and flying controls could be positioned in the best locations. Wooden replicas of the controls were attached to ropes to represent the control cables and all the levers and switches were tested in numerous positions until the optimal arrangement was found. Even the possibility of reflections was studied, and mirrors were fitted in place of the cockpit windows so that all manner of reflections and glare could be explored in detail before the design was fixed. But despite their efforts, they failed to consider the nose-mounted landing light, which was later found to be very troublesome in fog, snow and cloud, when it could often blind the crew. However, they did ensure that the flight deck was rain-proof and as draft-proof as possible, and also designed the cockpit windows so that the pilot could reach outside and clean them when necessary.

Inside the main cabin, attention was paid to the problem of noise that had plagued so many early commercial aircraft. Piston engines produced a great deal of noise and vibration, and when this was

A magnificent photograph of NC15599, pictured wearing the livery of Eastern Airlines. After joining the airline in 1940, this particular DC-3 was eventually resold and finally ended its flying days on January 4, 1976, when an engine failure led to a wheels-up landing at Corpus Christie in Texas. (Tim McLelland collection)

combined with the effect of propellers, the results could be astonishingly loud, the Ford Tri-Motor recording some 100 decibels inside its cabin. Sperry's Dr. Stephen Zand had completed some research into the issue and his findings were applied to the new DC-1. Various materials were investigated as possible sound insulation, and eventually he recommended "Seapak," comprising of several layers of Kapok laid against the aircraft's aluminum skin, together with a layer of filter material. Stretched fabric and paneling (made from rubber and balsa wood) then covered the Seapak, and this reduced the DC-1's cabin sound levels to a respectable 72 decibels at 185mph, reducing to 65 at 90mph, which was less than inside the flight deck. The sound insulation also contributed towards better internal temperatures, and a new heating system was developed for the aircraft. Heat was drawn from the engines and applied to a small, corrugated steel boiler to produce thermostatically controlled steam heat. Next to each passenger seat a self-adjusting cool air inlet was fitted and air ducts from the aircraft's nose were linked to grills in the cabin floor that provided draft-free ventilation. This provided a complete change of internal air every minute and when combined with the heating system it maintained a cabin temperature of 70 degrees even when the outside air temperature was below zero. Douglas produced promotional literature that extolled the virtues of the DC-1's excellent noise, vibration and temperature levels, claiming that air sickness in the aircraft would be "practically unknown," although the causes of sickness obviously had

Delivered in 1940 to Eastern Airlines, NC28391 was sold to Trans Texas Airlines during the late 1940s. Unlike many of its counterparts, it was not impressed into USAAF service from 1941–45, but probably performed cargo transport duties within the US during that period. (Eddie Coates collection)

little to do with such facilities. But even if Douglas could not cure air sickness, the DC-1 was to become the quietest and most comfortable passenger aircraft yet built.

Construction of the first DC-1 began on March 15, 1953. The precise design of the airframe had changed quite significantly by this stage as the predicted weight increased and the center-of-gravity moved rearwards. The planned span of the wings had been set at 80ft, but this was increased to 85ft when the wing was swept backwards (the trailing edge remaining straight) in order to counter the shift in the center-of-gravity, this change being deemed much easier than moving the entire wing structure backwards. This revision gave the aircraft a satisfactory performance on just one engine, even though some of the Douglas team still worried that if the aircraft grew any heavier it would not be capable of flying at all. Raymond remained confident that the DC-1 would perform well, thanks to the new controllable pitch propeller that was being developed by Hamilton Standard. This new innovation would enable the pilot to increase the propeller's pitch for take-off (providing greater torque) and would be more efficient at higher altitudes and Raymond commented that it would "bail us out" if the weight problem became more of a concern. Two engine companies were assigned to the project, with the Wright Engine Company positioned on one side of the DC-1 production line, while Pratt & Whitney occupied a space on the other side, both being separated from each other by large screens. Both teams worked frantically in close proximity, despite maintaining complete separation from each other, without so much as a conversation between them. It was clear from the outset that the new aircraft would reward the aircraft's engine manufacturer with a very lucrative contract, and so both companies struggled to create the most suitable and affordable powerplant. Wright eventually emerged victorious with their Cyclone engine, although Pratt & Whitney eventually created its competing Wasp engine a couple of years later, and although the majority of the early aircraft were fitted with Wright engines, Pratt & Whitney ultimately succeeded in becoming the main manufacturer of engines for the DC-1's later variants.

It was on June 22, 1933, that the first DC-1 X223Y emerged from its hangar at Clover Field. It was one of the largest aircraft to have ever been built at that time and with its sleek, silver fuselage, mighty radial engines (each of which produced more power than all three of the engines fitted to the aged Tri-Motors) and large passenger windows, it undoubtedly looked impressive, even though some observers wondered if it was too big to fly. In fact, it was already expected to be more than capable of exceeding the requirements that had been laid down by TWA, and in retrospect it might be argued that the DC-1 was over-engineered. Raymond stated: "The absence of sophisticated tests for stress on parts and limited experience with all-metal design may have led us to pick stronger materials than we needed. We didn't go about it to make it conservative, we wanted to make it safe, and there was not much experience with design." This policy proved to be the foundation of the DC-2 and DC-3 aircraft's success and explains why surviving examples of the DC-3 family would still be in use a staggering 80 years after the type's first flight. On July 1, the aircraft was declared ready for its first flight and arrangements were made to fly during the company's lunch break so that the Douglas employees could see the historic event. Chief test pilot Carl Cover was accompanied by copilot Fred Herman, and together they started-up the DC-1's engines and taxied the aircraft out onto the landing field for a high-speed run. Cover then brought the aircraft back along the runway, turned back into wind and at 12.36 the DC-1 roared into life again and began its first take-off run, accompanied by cheers from the 800-strong crowd and a comment from Donald Douglas that "she's off." The initial thrill of seeing the DC-1 get airborne did not last long, and just seconds later the port engine began to lose power, swiftly followed by the starboard engine. As the aircraft headed out towards the Pacific Ocean, it began to sink as Cover hauled the aircraft into a left turn. It disappeared out of sight and the crowd feared the worst, but it reappeared as the crew coaxed a little height out of the struggling engines. It then sank again but recovered, eventually reaching 1,000ft at which stage Cover concluded that the aircraft needed to be put back on the ground as swiftly as possible, and just 12 minutes after take-off he carefully put the aircraft back onto the runway and taxied back to the hangar. It looked as if contaminated fuel had caused the engines to fail and days of careful inspection followed, but no obvious cause was found. Cover had a hunch that the engine carburetors were to blame, and after some reluctance from the Wright Company's engineers, they were inspected in some detail. It then became obvious that it was their backwards mounting arrangement that had caused the problem, causing fuel flow to be cut off from the engines when the aircraft entered a nose-up attitude. The solution was to simply remount them facing forwards and on July 7, the DC-1 flew again, and the engines performed flawlessly. Unfortunately, the airframe did not perform quite so well, and it yawed violently from side to side as it lumbered over the Californian

Although the DC-3 quickly replaced the earlier DC-2 in commercial service, the earlier model remained active around the world for many years. Eight DC-2s were captured by Germany during World War Two, including NA:LA 1366, formerly operated by KLM as PH-AKT. (*Aeroplane* collection)

countryside. The aircraft was returned to the Douglas hangar and the rudder linkage was modified, while the actual surface of the rudder was flattened and increased in surface area. When it flew again the aircraft showed no further handling vices and more thorough flight testing began.

The DC-1's testing was thorough and more exhaustive than anything that had been applied to other commercial aircraft, but the DC-1 performed well, and the Douglas team was soon encouraged to perform what was perhaps the most crucial test and fly the aircraft on one engine. This would prove the aircraft's ability to meet TWA's performance stipulations and if it failed, it would effectively scupper the aircraft's future. September 12 saw the aircraft prepared for its critical test, loaded with water ballast to bring it up to a representative operational weight and set for a long flight over Winslow in Arizona, where an altitude of 4,256ft was combined with routinely high temperatures of around 100 degrees. The initial take-off run was uneventful, and as the DC-1 prepared to lift into the air, test pilot Eddie Allen called for the landing gear to be retracted so that additional drag on the airframe would be reduced as quickly as possible. He then shut down the starboard engine. However, Allen had slightly mis-timed his command for gear retraction and when the undercarriage began to retract the wings had yet to generate a safe amount of lift, and the DC-1 struggled to stay airborne, the spinning propellers almost clipping the runway. Thankfully, Allen's huge flying experience enabled him to keep the aircraft from disaster, and as speed gradually built up, the aircraft began to gently climb and begin its two-hour journey to Albuquerque in New Mexico, where it landed without ceremony and soon returned in a more conventional manner to Clover Field. With this critical exercise completed to TWA's satisfaction, the DC-1 was accepted for commercial use and on September 13, 1933, it entered service with TWA. Almost all of the flight testing had been completed without major problems, and the aircraft had survived a great deal of very demanding flying. Throughout this period the DC-1 suffered only one relatively minor accident when it landed on its belly following a breakdown of communications between the on-board crew. The person who had been expected to lower the landing gear (in this instance it was Oswald), was diverted to assist with observation of the tail wheel's behavior, and pilots Allen and Tomlinson failed to notice that the gear had not been extended as planned. The DC-1 scraped along the grass runway and came to a halt with bent propellers and a badly dented fuselage skin along the underside. But despite this potentially disastrous landing, the aircraft's

The US Civil Aeronautics Administration acquired its first DC-3 in 1941, and many DC-3 (and C-47) aircraft were subsequently flown by the administration. NC815 is pictured during Goodyear/CAA crosswind landing wheel and tire tests that involved the use of specially modified castering wheel units. The aircraft's registration number has been modified with tape to become "NX815" for these trials. (Tim McLelland collection)

This DC-3 was manufactured as aircraft No. 6264. It was allocated the US registration NC33680, but it did not enter into commercial service in this guise. Instead, it was transferred to the USAAF as a C-49J transport, serial 43-1981. After World War Two, it finally resumed its commercial role with TWA as NC30079. (Aeroplane collection)

structure was intact, and the DC-1 was swiftly repaired. Donald Douglas did not apportion blame for the incident and simply arranged for the aircraft to be fixed. Oswald (who was technically responsible for the damage) later said that he had wanted the DC-1 design to feature full landing gear retraction, but the partially-extended configuration employed on the aircraft had proved to be a very useful safety feature, enabling the aircraft to land intact even when its undercarriage was raised.

United Airlines NC16063 pictured as the aircraft roars over the perimeter road at Oakland Airport in California, during 1940. (Bill Larkins)

DC-3A-197 NC16072 (c/n 1912) was delivered to United Air Lines and named *State of California*. It enjoyed only a brief flying career before being destroyed in a hangar fire at Salt Lake City Municipal Airport on January 12, 1941. (Tim McLelland collection)

NC33609 was completed as a DC-3A-228F, n/n 4100. Delivered to Pan American Airways on May 7, 1941, it was operated by that company until 1946 when it was sold to Cubana, registered as CU-T38. It was sold again in 1962 and was probably scrapped during the early 1970s. (Tim McLelland collection)

Wearing the flamboyant markings of Pan American Airways (PAA), NC30091 was manufactured as a C-53D during World War Two, scheduled for service with the USAAF as 42-68847. However, it was delivered to PAA in September 1943 and remained in use with PAA until the early 1950s. (Eddie Coates Collection)

Manufactured as a C-53D (42-68718), NC44883 joined Continental Airlines after World War Two. Continental replaced its fleet of Lockheed Lodestars with DC-3s during 1948. Named *City of Denver*, the aircraft is pictured at Denver's Stapleton Airport late in 1947. (Eddie Coates collection)

Continental modified its airline livery during the early 1950s. Two Continental DC-3s are seen here at Stapleton Airport in 1956. N68719 was a former USAAF C-53 (41-20073), which was eventually sold to Ford as an executive transport. In the background is N15585, a former C-47 that was withdrawn from USAAF service in 1944 before joining Continental. (Eddie Coates collection)

Built for the USAAF as a C-53D, 42-68792 was purchased by United and became NC44995. After various resales, the aircraft went to Mexico and was still active long after 2000. (Eddie Coates collection)

N877MG was built as a C-47 during World War Two and delivered to the China National Aviation Corporation (CNAC), flying "The Hump" on the India–Burma–China routes. The aircraft continued service until 1949, when the Chinese civil war broke out. After years of ownership dispute, the aircraft returned to the US and converted to Super DC-3 configuration with more powerful engines and extended-range auxiliary fuel tanks. Serving as the corporate aircraft for Johnson and Johnson, ownership then changed many times before acquisition by the Historic Flight Foundation (HFF) in 2007. Now fully restored to represent a PAA DC-3 from 1949, the HFF continues to own and operate the aircraft. (James Polivka)

Pictured in the markings of Qantas during 1958, VH-EBU was manufactured as a C-47 with American serial 42-92392. It was delivered to the Royal Air Force (RAF) as FZ631 and subsequently sold to Qantas. It was eventually resold to Trans Australian Airlines and continued flying until 2008, at which stage it was scrapped. (R. A. Scholefield collection)

Wisconsin Central became North Central Airlines in 1952. DC-3 N38943 served with the airline for some time but was eventually resold, and the aircraft ended its days in Florida, where it was finally impounded after having been involved in illegal drug runs during the 1970s. (Eddie Coates collection)

Delivered to the USAAF in 1941, C-47-DL 41-18352 quickly became civilianized and joined Braniff International Airways. It is seen at Chicago's Miday Airport prior to being sold to Lake Central Airlines. (Eddie Coates collection)

The flamboyant markings of Air France adorn DC-3 F-BCYV as the aircraft prepares to embark on a night flight. This aircraft remained in France for much of its active life and was still flying with Vargas Aviation in the late 1970s with most of its Air France livery still intact. (Tim McLelland collection)

Chapter 5

Into Service

TWA were immediately impressed with the new DC-1, and it surpassed all of the company's hopes and expectations. Such was the delight with the aircraft that an order was swiftly placed for 20 more machines and Douglas drew up plans for production. Some minor changes to the aircraft were proposed but setting up the aircraft for series production required completely new drawings, a new mock-up airframe and new production tooling. Perhaps most significantly, the development of Wright's engines had reached a stage where a new 855hp powerplant could be introduced, and this would enable Douglas to stretch the DC-1s fuselage in order to create additional capacity. But making this change would affect the aircraft's center-of-gravity, and so the wing structure would also have to be shifted. All of these changes effectively created a significantly different machine, even though it retained the basic design and structure of the DC-1, but Douglas believed that the changes were sufficiently significant to rename the production-standard machine as the DC-2.

Although much of the DC-1's initial development and testing had been done, manufacturing the DC-2 was a very significant risk for Douglas, bearing in mind that the DC-1 had already cost the company some US$350,000. The new contract with TWA promised a price of $65,000 for each aircraft (excluding engines), but further orders would be vital if the company was to recover the costs of the DC-1 and the first batch of DC-2s. Thankfully, orders were forthcoming and production of the DC-2 continued after the fleet of 20 aircraft was manufactured for TWA. The first DC-2 was delivered to TWA on May 14, 1934, and four days later it completed its first passenger flight from Columbus to Newark via Pittsburgh. Eastern Airlines ordered a batch of 14 aircraft and Pan American Airways ordered 16, while Dutch operator KLM ordered two and became the first European operator of the type, subsequently purchasing a further 18 aircraft. It was KLM that brought the DC-2 to the attention of a worldwide audience, when one of its fleet (PH-AJU) was entered into the 1934 MacRobertson Air Race from London to Melbourne in Australia. With the DC-2 already in service with TWA, United Airlines struggled to maintain its customer base with its fleet of Boeing 247s. The new DC-2 was faster than the 247, and it was a much more comfortable aircraft to fly in, thanks to its much roomier cabin and much lower noise levels. Despite spending more than a million dollars to upgrade

July 2010 and the DC-3's 75th anniversary is celebrated in style at Whiteside County Airport in Illinois. No less than 26 active DC-3s (and a DC-2) are present. (Trev Morson, DouglasDC3.com)

the 247s, passengers voted with their feet and chose the DC-2, and United Airlines began to accept that the DC-2 was unbeatable. United decided to enter a 247 in the MacRobertson race but the decision proved to be a disaster for both the airline and the 247. As expected, the specially designed de Havilland Comet racing plane won the race but KLM's DC-2 came second, much to everyone's surprise, especially when the DC-2 flew an additional 1,000 miles more than the stipulated racecourse and carried seven people, together with 421lb of mail, and even completed no less than 13 stops en route. Nobody had imagined that a commercial airliner would achieve an overall time that was only 34 minutes less than the winning design that was (at that time) the fastest aircraft in Europe, and one that had been specifically built for the race. The *London Morning Post*'s writer stated:

> The results of the England–Australia air race have fallen like a bomb in the midst of British everyday commercial and military aviation. Pre-conceived ideas of the maximum speed limitations of standard commercial aeroplanes have been blown sky high. British standard aeroplane development, both commercial and military, has been standing still. America now has standard commercial aeroplanes than the fastest aeroplane in regular service in any squadron in the whole of the Royal Air Force.

The once futuristic Boeing 247 finished the race in third place, more than 22 hours behind the DC-2. It was inevitable that public and commercial perception of the 247 would reflect its performance in the air race, and it was subsequently regarded as being clearly inferior to the DC-2, and the DC-2's success was thereby assured. Douglas anticipated producing 50 aircraft but within months the order book was at 75 and by the time that production of the DC-2 ended, some 21 overseas airlines had purchased the aircraft, together with those in the continental USA. One of the most important

The main cabin of C-47 G-AMRA was fitted out for passenger flying, but its military origins remained all too clear. (Air Atlantique)

DC-3A-197 NC16072 enjoyed only a very brief active life. After joining United Air Lines in 1936, the aircraft was destroyed in a hangar fire at Salt Lake City Airport in January 1941 (together with a Boeing 247 from Western Air Express). (R. A. Scholefield collection)

developments for Douglas was the involvement of European manufacturer Fokker, a company that had traditionally supplied aircraft to KLM. When Tony Fokker first learned of KLM's intention to buy the DC-2, he approached Douglas to set up a license production arrangement so that Fokker could manufacture the DC-2 within Europe. The result was a lucrative arrangement for both Fokker and Douglas, but it was tinged with regret for Fokker, a company that had previously held such a strong position within the industry as designer and manufacturer of its own aircraft. Spanish airline Lineas Postales Espanolas ordered five DC-2s and took delivery of the sole surviving DC-1, and three of these machines later became involved in the Spanish Civil War, converted into gun platforms and bombers. Poland's Polskie Linie Lotnicze purchased two DC-2s, opting to refit them with British engines. Perhaps not surprisingly, the USSR also purchased just one DC-2 but immediately embarked on a project to copy the airframe's design, remanufacturing the aircraft (without any license agreement) as the ANT-35. Even further afield, Nakajima Hikoki KK obtained rights to build the DC-2 under license in Japan, purchasing one assembled airframe and five unassembled aircraft. Designated as the AT-2 and later the Ki-34, these were assigned to the Japan Air Transport Company (which subsequently became Japan Airlines) in 1936. China's Canton Airlines and the China National Aviation Corporation both purchased a pair of DC-2s and CNAC eventually merged with Pan American Airways (PAA), acquiring more DC-2s from PAA as part of the process. Back in the United Kingdom, Airspeed obtained an agreement to manufacture the DC-2 for British sales, but the combination of a severely depressed economy, and the looming threat of war with Germany was enough to prevent production from ever getting underway. Likewise, a similar plan in France was suffering the same fate, Louis Renault having proposed to manufacture the DC-2 with (in typical French fashion) his own 600hp engines. Back in the United States, the DC-2 also captured the imagination of the private business market, and aircraft were manufactured for a variety of companies, all of whom appreciated the aircraft's outstanding performance and (by contemporary standards) luxurious comfort.

It's interesting to note that the DC-2 was greatly admired for the standards of comfort afforded to its passengers. Gone were the days of smelling salts and cotton wool ear plugs, and a new age of

A fascinating close-up look at a C-47 in flight, illustrating the flight deck escape hatch, the wind screen washer and wiper system, and the sliding side window. (Air Atlantique)

spaciousness, flight attendants and even in-flight movies had dawned. But when the DC-2 is compared to airliners of the present day, it is important to appreciate that conditions were, to say the least, surprisingly basic, especially for crews. Pilots regularly flew with the flight deck side windows open so that the ever-present smells of hot oil and fuel, and vomit (if conditions were bumpy), could be reduced. Conditions in the cockpit were often either stiflingly hot or freezing cold, and to make matters worse the DC-2's windshield often leaked so that flying through rain often ensured a soaking for the crew. However, in terms of handling, the DC-2 was regarded as a good aircraft to fly, possessing few vices. The only persistent criticism leveled at the aircraft was the very rigid nature of the landing gear, which resulted in disturbingly heavy landings, even though the sturdy airframe easily absorbed the shock. In fact, more than a few landings resulted in the collapse of the undercarriage, but the incredibly tough DC-3 took such incidents in its stride, even if the aircraft's passengers did not. Another criticism of the undercarriage was the ground steering system that relied upon the use of a heavy brake actuating handle and the judicious use of the rudder pedals. The result was an unavoidable lag between application and effect, and more than a few pilots found themselves in embarrassing circumstances when the steering system defeated them. Likewise, the landing gear had to be raised and lowered by hand pump, and even in the best of conditions it required a minute's work to retract the wheels, while in particularly cold conditions it was sometimes almost impossible to raise the gear at all, and some pilots resorted to beginning the pumping sequence before the aircraft had even left the ground. The cabin's steam heating system also became notoriously troublesome, despite being designed with simplicity in mind. The copilot was tasked with the continual balancing of the system's water valves, but in practice the copilot often found himself devoting more time to the heating system than flying the aircraft. The valves and pipes hissed, gurgled and rattled, and occasionally treated passengers to foul-smelling vapor, but despite its shortcomings, the system was a major improvement over anything that had hitherto been provided for passengers. Even with its relatively minor vices, the DC-2 was a major step forward in commercial design, and its robust construction, comfortable layout and significantly lower operating costs ensured that the aircraft became a worldwide phenomenon.

Scientific American published a glowing report on the DC-2's success:

The DC-2 put American commercial aviation years ahead of Europe. The airlines, faced with decreasing revenues from the mails, and with competition from the railroads, showed great wisdom in not merely stepping up the speed of their service. With the DC-2 they made conscious efforts to make every trip comfortable for the passenger. When a traveller boarded the plane, a friendly flight attendant, or copilot, handed the passenger a little package containing chewing gum, and cotton for his ears. With the improvement in noise elimination in the DC-2 the cotton soon became an artifact.

By 1934, the DC-2 was assigned to 27 percent of all the air miles flown in the continental USA, even though only 42 aircraft were then in use, representing just 7.5 percent of the total number of aircraft in service. Donald Douglas exhibited his pride in the DC-2 by inviting his parents to fly in the aircraft, and they could offer only praise to their son for producing such a magnificent aircraft. Privately

Completed as a C-47-DL for the United States Army Air Force (USAAF) as 41-18679, this particular aircraft was delivered to Canadian Pacific as CF-CPX. It remained active in Canada for some time before moving to the US register as N8061A. It is believed to be still active and based in Mississippi. (R. A. Scholefield collection)

however, his father teased Donald, saying that "It was a great ride but my back felt broken for two days after the trip. It almost finished me off." Cyrus Smith, the President of American Airlines and Vice President of Engineering William Littlewood, also both flew in the DC-2 and like William Douglas, they were greatly impressed, despite having some reservations over the aircraft's performance. Most importantly, they believed that it lacked power, and even though it was faster than any other airliner, it still could not complete the New York to Chicago route without a stopover. They also received reports from pilots that the DC-2 suffered from some minor handling problems such as heavy flying controls and some directional instability, plus some problems with icing on the propellers and fin. Douglas devised some modifications to solve these difficulties, but Smith and Littlewood believed that the logical way to create a near-perfect aircraft would be to design what would, in effect, be a new aircraft, based on the DC-2 airframe. Littlewood drew up some basic plans of the aircraft that they felt would be ideal for American Airlines, and eventually they invited Arthur Raymond to look at the drawings and offer his own input. The result was Douglas Aircraft Report No. 1004, which outlined in some detail the requirements that American Airlines had laid down. The proposed aircraft was still very much a DC-2 but substantially bigger, chiefly because American Airlines wanted an overnight sleeper aircraft for longer routes. Smith telephoned Donald Douglas to discuss the report and although Douglas agreed to examine the proposal, he was less than enthusiastic about the idea. With some 102 DC-2s already manufactured and another 90 aircraft in production, creating a new version of the aircraft would require more design work, new tooling, and more money. Smith persisted with his argument that a new design would be advantageous not only for American Airlines but Douglas too, and, after spending US$300 on his two-hour telephone call, Donald Douglas finally accepted that he should develop the DC-2 into a more ambitious design, tailored to Smith's requirements.

Chicago and Southern Air Lines emerged from Pacific Seaboard Air Lines, which formed in 1935. One of many early operators of the DC-3, the airline merged with Delta Airlines in 1935. (R. A. Scholefield collection)

DC-3 VH-AVM was leased to Australian National Airways (ANA) between 1950 and 1953. Built as a C-47A-30-DL (USAAF serial 42-23728) it was operated by the Royal Australian Air Force (RAAF) during World War Two as A65-10. After six years of service with Guinea Airways and ANA, it was sold to Meteor Air Transport New Jersey as N1433V. (R. A. Scholefield collection)

Built in 1943 as a C-53D-DO and delivered to the USAAF as 42-68711, this aircraft was subsequently registered to DNL as LN-IAI and named *Nordis* in March 1946. It operated the first international service for DNL after the war, on the Oslo–Copenhagen route. Transferred to SAS in 1948, it was later renamed *Einar Viking* and reregistered as LN-IKI in 1949. (Eddie Coates collection)

Western Air Lines operated a small fleet of DC-3s and Boeing 247s during the early 1940s, the company being formed following the ending of an interchange arrangement between Western Air Express and United Airlines. This vintage illustration shows the company's rather basic support facilities that were far from suitable for what was (at that time) a large and advanced passenger transport. (Eddie Coates collection)

Constructed as a DC3-313 during 1939, NC21782 is pictured whilst operating with Capital Airways. Seventy years later, the aircraft is still airworthy, but currently unlicensed, with M.J. Supply Inc. in Colorado. (Eddie Coates collection)

Braniff International acquired its first DC-3s in 1939. However, most of the airline's fleet was handed to the US Defense Department when World War Two began and at one stage the airline had only 147 available passenger seats for the whole company. DC-3 operations continued after the war until the type was gradually replaced by the DC-6. (Eddie Coates collection)

DC-3 EI-ACI (c/n 9036) joined Aer Lingus in December 1945 and continued to operate with the airline until March 1959, named as *St. Aidan*. Prior to commercial service, the aircraft flew with the USAAF as 42-32810. (Tim McLelland collection)

A magnificent image of the Trans Texas Airways facility at Houston during 1950, showing DC-3s in various states of overhaul. After this photograph was taken, the airline developed their company livery into a striking black and yellow scheme that was applied to its DC-3 fleet. (Eddie Coates collection)

Chapter 6
Bigger and Better

It has often been claimed that if Smith had not been so enthusiastic, Donald Douglas would never have agreed to proceed with the proposal. It is undoubtedly true that Douglas remained skeptical, as he could not see any logical need for a sleeper aircraft, given that the very notion of sleeping in an airliner was almost absurd. The uncomfortable and noisy Condors and Tri-Motors were barely tolerable for shorter daytime flights, and the idea of attempting to sleep in an airliner seemed almost ludicrous to Douglas, and he could not believe that American Airlines would be prepared to finance the concept. However, Cyrus Smith took advantage of a loan facility that had been made available by the US government in response to the Great Depression. He obtained money from the Reconstruction Finance Agency and used this to fund the development of the new Douglas aircraft, and on July 8, 1935, he ordered ten aircraft at a cost of US$795,000 (this order later doubled). Surprisingly, Smith did not sign a contract for the aircraft until April 8, 1936, and until that date the design and manufacturing process continued only on the basis of the telegram in which Smith had placed the initial order. Such was Smith's confidence in Douglas that he simply did not see any need to sign a contract, and Douglas later praised Smith during the Newcomen Society's annual dinner in 1955:

> This is an ideal time to acknowledge our debt of gratitude to my good friend C. R. Smith, for his part in the development of the DC-3. He had tremendous faith in us, and in the future of air travel. His boundless energy, clear vision, and uncanny knack of making the right decision at the right time were the catalytic agents that greatly influenced us in taking steps to build that famous airplane.

Littlewood accepted that Douglas would be reluctant to create a completely new aircraft, and so he based his design projection on the existing DC-2, altering the structure only where necessary. He was assured by Curtiss-Wright that its 855hp engine could be improved to deliver 1,000hp, and this increase in power enabled him to draw up a wider and rounder fuselage that would more easily accommodate sleeping berths. Douglas calculated that the reshaped fuselage would retain the DC-2's center section structure and outer wing panels, but that it would require a slightly larger cockpit section and a more generous tail surface. They estimated that even with these changes the new aircraft could retain roughly 80 percent of the DC-2 design, but it soon became clear that even with minimal changes, they would in effect be creating a very different machine.

Raymond recalled:

> [That the Douglas team] gave Bill Littlewood almost a free hand in establishing the dimensions of the cabin, and deciding what went into the cockpit layout. We worked together without any friction. The DC-3 was a product of teamwork. This was the primary reason why it was so successful. They could have built it themselves if they could do it in-house, but my relationship with Bill and our relationship with the American Airlines people influenced that plane a lot. Conceptually the DC-3 design was easy. In reality however, we spent more than half our time in the shop, and we had over 400 engineers and draftsmen working on the design. We spent many long nights producing more than 3,500 drawings, but it was worth it.

Built for Eastern Airlines, the aircraft went to the USAAF as C-49K 43-2007 in December 1942. After serving in Alaska, it went to TWA in May 1944 before being acquired by Wisconsin Central Airlines in February 1951. It joined North Central in December 1952 and continued to fly with various smaller operators until 1987, when it was severely damaged by a Tornado in Texas. (Tim McLelland collection)

G-AJHZ was a former BEA C-47, acquired by South Coast Air Services, a small and short-lived company primarily connected with cargo services. (Barry Friend)

G-AMPZ was a former RAF C-47 (KN442), operated by various companies including Rig Air (which eventually became Air Anglia). It eventually joined Air Atlantique and was written off in a forced landing in 2010 during a passenger flight commemorating the Berlin Airlift. (Barry Friend)

C-47 G-ANTD enjoyed a long life with various companies in the UK, beginning with Derby Airways, based at Burnaston (now the site of a huge Toyota car factory) near Derby. This small airline became British Midland in 1964 and G-ANTD soon acquired the airline's new livery. It was also operated by Air Anglia from Norwich Airport, and the aircraft was finally grounded and scrapped during 1973. (Barry Friend)

Formed in 1960 as a result of a merger between Airwork Services and Hunting Clan Air Transport, British United Airways (BUA) operated a mixed fleet of airliners, including a number of DC-3 and C-47s. G-ANTB illustrates the company's first livery, which was replaced from 1966 onwards, as illustrated by G-AKNB. (Barry Friend)

C-47 G-AGHM is pictured here in the colors of Cambrian Airways. As can be seen, the early post-war livery was eventually replaced by a more modern and more flamboyant paint scheme. Unusually, G-AGHM eventually ended its days in the Middle East, and after withdrawal from use, the aircraft was placed on permanent display in the middle of a roundabout in Jeddah. (Barry Friend)

Morton Air Services was one of the first post-war independent British airlines to be formed. Equipped with a variety of aircraft including the C-47, the company operated domestic and European services from Croydon Airport, and it was one of this company's aircraft (a Heron) that conducted the very last passenger flight from Croydon in 1959. The company was absorbed by BUIA during the 1960s. (Barry Friend)

G-AOGZ was formerly the RAF's KN628 – the personal transport of Field Marshal Montgomery. It joined Derby Aviation in 1954 before being sold to Strathair, which leased the aircraft to both Cirrus Aviation and Emerald Air. It eventually returned to the USA and after a further period of use it was withdrawn and scrapped in Florida. (Barry Friend)

C-47 G-ALXK (c/n 32828) joined Dan-Air during 1964 and flew with the airline for two years before being withdrawn. It was stored at Lasham for some time (as illustrated) before being scrapped there in 1969. (Barry Friend)

 Indeed, American Airlines flew many of its engineers to Santa Monica so that they could work directly with Douglas engineers on designing the cabin berth layout. Cyrus Smith also provided a great deal of input, and it was he who proposed the concept of building a door into the rear of the starboard fuselage. Until now, most airlines had usually catered for doors on the port side of aircraft, but American Airlines had facilities to accommodate the right-hand door fitted in their Ford Tri-Motors. However, Smith was more concerned with passenger comfort, and he had observed that pilots normally started up an aircraft's port engine first, therefore it seemed logical to allow passengers to enter the aircraft from the starboard side, so that they were not buffeted by the prop wash of a running engine. The finished design looked much the same as the DC-2, but the new DC-3 was substantially larger with a longer and wider fuselage, a wider wingspan, greater tail area, more powerful engines, and a stronger landing gear assembly. Despite maintaining much of the DC-2's overall configuration, the emerging DC-3 eventually shared little more than ten percent commonality with its predecessor. Raymond explained: "There was plenty of data from the DC-1 and DC-2 to formulate the design. Often, we got down on the floor and worked things out ourselves. There was personal ingenuity and application, and we made things happen overnight." Initially, the new design was referred to as the DST –Douglas Sleeper Transport, and was described by Douglas as follows:

Wings: Wings are of cantilever, internally braced, multi-spar, stressed skin type construction consisting of formed aluminum alloy sheet and extruded members riveted and bolted together. They are made in three sections, i.e., the center section of constant chord to which engine nacelles are attached, and the right and left hand outer tapered wing panels. A series of progressive high-lift airfoils are used outward to the wing tip. Each outer wing panel consists of a main section, a detachable trailing edge section at the inboard end, and a detachable wing tip. The aft portion of the underside of the wing is provided with hydraulically operated split trailing edge flaps. The ailerons consist of an aluminum alloy riveted framework covered with fabric. They are cable actuated. The right aileron is provided with a cable-actuated trim tab. The center section and each outer wing panel have three spars. Pressed aluminum alloy ribs, made in sections, and aluminum lateral stringers comprise the wing structure. Steel fittings are used where the imposed loads make their use mandatory.

Empennage: Multi-cellular construction of formed aluminum alloy sheet and extrusions is used in the cantilever, internally braced, horizontal and vertical stabilizers. These surfaces are attached in a fixed alignment to the fuselage. The rudder and elevator are of aluminum alloy riveted framework covered with fabric. Each rudder and elevator is statically and dynamically balanced and is also provided with a cable actuated trim tab.

Fuselage: The fuselage is of all-metal, semi-monocoque construction, almost circular in section and built up of channel-section transverse frames, or formers, and extruded bulb angle stringers. The framework is made of aluminum alloy sheets, extrusions, and rolled structural members all riveted and bolted together. Transverse frames are riveted to longitudinal stringers. Alclad 24-ST aluminum alloy of various gauges covers the fuselage framework and is joined to it with snap rivets. The fuselage is subdivided into the pilot's compartment, right and left forward cargo compartments, main cabin and a lavatory aft of the entrance door.

Landing Gear: Landing gear consists of two independent wheel units, located under an engine nacelle and attached to the primary spar of the center section of the wing. The hydraulically actuated landing gear can be retracted into the engine nacelles, the lower part of each wheel projects. In order to make possible landings at normal sinking speed, four hydro-pneumatic shock absorber struts are provided. These struts, in conjunction with balloon tires and hydraulically actuated servo-type brakes, make it possible to operate from fields with rough runways or limited length. Each landing gear unit retracts individually. The tail wheel does not retract and is capable of swiveling 360 degrees. During take-off or landing operations, tail wheel is locked in a fore and aft position.

Engine Installation: Two Wright Cyclone 1,000 hp radial air-cooled engines are installed. Each engine is enclosed in a cowl and may be quickly removed with the accessories and relevant piping intact by means of quick-disconnect fittings on each line at the firewall in the engine nacelle.

Propellers: In order to provide maximum propulsive efficiency and better cooling to the engines, paddle blade propellers have been used with success. These propellers are Hamilton Standard, Quick-Feathering, Hydromatic and constant speed types, and are controllable in blade pitch setting.

Fuel System: The fuel system consists of four aluminum alloy fuel tanks, which are located within the center section of the wing. Each engine gets its fuel supply by means of a separate piping system, fuel selector and cross-feed fuel valves. Fuel can be directed to supply either engine or to either engine-driven fuel pump when necessary. For emergency use, two auxiliary, manually operated fuel pumps are available for use by the pilot.

Engine Oil System: An independent oil system is provided for each engine. Lubrication oil is contained in a tank inside the engine nacelle over the landing gear. Hot lubricating engine oil is cooled by means of an oil cooler attached to the underside of each engine nacelle. To facilitate engine starting in cold weather, each oil tank is provided with an oil dilution system.

Hydraulic System: Landing gear, brakes, wing flaps, cowl flaps, and automatic pilot controls are actuated by means of hydraulic power generated by two engine-driven hydraulic pumps supplying energy to the hydraulic system. During normal operations, one pump and its relevant system supplies power to all the movable components, other than the automatic pilot. The automatic pilot is operated by the other hydraulic system, but it is possible to use either system to perform similar functions by means of a selector valve. For auxiliary use, a hydraulic fluid hand pump is available.

Flight Controls: A conventional yoke, column, and rudder pedals which by means of cables, actuates the flight control systems, and control surfaces, is provided for the pilot and copilot. Aileron, elevator, and rudder trim tabs are controlled as to setting from the pilot's compartment, and are also actuated by means of cables. The automatic pilot controls the movement of the rudders, ailerons, and elevators in order to maintain directional, lateral and longitudinal stability in flight.

Electrical: Two engine-driven generators provide electrical energy to the 24-volt ground return electrical system. Two large ampere-hour storage batteries are stowed within the fuselage after it flows through a heat exchanger attached to the engine exhaust manifold. Regulation of the volume and the temperature of the warm air can be controlled by the pilot.

Ice Elimination System: Elimination of ice from the leading edge of the airfoil surfaces is accomplished by means of rubber de-ice boots, that are attached to the wings and tail surfaces. The inflation of the de-ice boots is done by engine driven vacuum pumps energizing a pneumatic system to inflate and deflate the de-ice boots periodically.

Internally, the DST was carefully configured precisely to the requirements of American Airlines. The passenger cabin was divided into eight sections, each of which contained two seats that could be converted into berths. Additional upper berths folded down from the upper fuselage and small additional windows were fixed into the fuselage to allow extra light into the compartments. Separate dressing rooms and toilets were located to the rear of the cabin and immediately behind the flight deck a VIP room was fitted, replicating the facilities found in Pullman rail cars of the period. Even the interior's color scheme was planned carefully so that a light and comfortable atmosphere was created, and some colors (particularly some shades of green) were avoided, as these had allegedly caused some passengers to suffer from air sickness, during tests that were conducted. Sound insulation reduced noise considerably, and the cabin floor was carpeted to add yet more insulation and a more general feeling of luxury. Following experience with the DC-2, the DST's landing gear was modified in order to avoid the "stiff legged" landings and bumpy take-off runs that inevitably jarred passengers. A new hydraulic system was combined with new shock absorbers, and a hydraulic pump was introduced to raise and lower the gear, which sped up the retraction sequence considerably and added to the aircraft's single engine safety. Because the gear was held into the engine bay recesses by hydraulic power, any loss of pressure resulted in the gear lowering automatically, so that there was little risk of the landing gear ever being locked up. Perhaps most importantly, the new DST was a better flying machine. The larger fuselage had indicated that an additional 5ft should be added to the outer wings, retaining the same wing plan as the DC-2. However, wind tunnel tests revealed that the extended

Formerly 43-15094, this DC-3 was operated by the Finnish Air Force and also flew with Aero Oy as OH-LCI. Pictured at Helsinki in 1969, it was sold in the US as N57NA and was eventually converted into a Basler BT-67, registered C-FMKB. (*Aeroplane*)

G-DAKS was part of the Aces High warbird fleet. It was repainted in fictional airline markings in 1982 as part of a television series. The registration, G-AGHY, was also fictional.

wing did not provide nearly as much lift as had been anticipated and it made the aircraft alarmingly unstable. Oswald recalled that "We tried dozens of models in the tunnel before we hit on the secret. We narrowed the airfoil, which changed the center of balance of the airplane resulting in the final wing design being enormously strong. The top skin was reinforced with corrugated sheeting with wrinkles running span-wise, strengthening the wing's capacity to withstand compression." Even so, the wing was still designed to flex under any significant load, and pilots often had to reassure passengers that the movement was normal, as few people had any experience of wings "flapping" in flight, until now. Other improvements over the DC-2 were less obvious but just as valuable. The wing's landing flaps had been operated by a laborious screw system on the DC-2, but new hydraulically operated surfaces were installed in the DST. Even the troublesome nose-mounted landing lights were changed, and new lights were incorporated into the wing leading edges, thereby solving the glare problem that manifested itself in some conditions.

The first completed DST was rolled-out without ceremony in December 1935. At that time, nobody regarded the DST as anything more than a development of an existing design, and so there was no appetite for a fuss. Even the first flight (made on December 17) was almost a non-event, and without so much as a hint of interest from the media, the DST (NX-14988 serial 1494) taxied out onto Clover Field on a cold and sunny afternoon, with Carl Cover at the controls with Frank Collbohm as copilot. Some five minutes were spent running the two Wright Cyclone SGR-1820-G-5 engines at full power, and then the aircraft positioned for take-off, and at 3pm the DST lumbered forwards and lifted into the air after a run of less than 1,000ft. In contrast to the DC-2's first flight, the DST performed faultlessly, and both Cover and Collbohm regarded the flight as entirely routine. Collbohm later commented that he "couldn't even remember whether it happened in the morning or afternoon. I can't separate it in my mind from any other test flights we made in those days." Nobody from the Douglas work force or management bothered to watch the first take-off, and with no company or media interest, nobody even bothered to photograph what eventually became recognized as one of the most iconic moments in the history of commercial aviation. After 90 minutes, the DST returned to Clover Field and the two-man crew reported that the aircraft had demonstrated no handling problems, although subsequent test flights revealed slightly inadequate directional stability, and a dorsal fillet was fitted ahead of the fin in order to cure this problem. The most worrying point in the DST's test program was during February 1936, at which stage the first aircraft had been refitted with developmental engines, as part of engine wear investigations. TWA was very interested in the aircraft and had requested a demonstration of the aircraft's capabilities. Much to everyone's surprise, the aircraft completed a long take-off run that was well in excess of 1,000ft, and this was unacceptable for TWA, who required aircraft that could operate comfortably from some very small landing fields. TWA decided to order DC-2s and the Douglas engineers were left to investigate the DST's flaw. Engine power was identified as the cause, and after the engines were dismantled, an oil ingestion problem inside the crankcases was discovered, and this had been causing the engines to run at high rpm, thereby reducing power output. Suitably repaired, the DST performed a shorter take-off of some 970ft, much to the relief of Douglas, and to the satisfaction of both TWA and American Airlines. But, by this stage, the DST's production schedule had been allocated to American and United Airlines, and they were forced to defer acceptance of any DC-3s until these initial orders had been completed. Pan American and Eastern Airlines quickly joined the order books, and the new aircraft's success was assured.

Delivered to the RAF as KN250, C-47 G-APBC subsequently joined Derby Airways, operating primarily from Burnaston. After further use in the UK, the aircraft went to Missionary Flight in Florida as N300MF at Fort Pierce. (David Whitworth/Tony Clarke collection)

Formerly Field Marshal Montgomery's personal transport KN628, C-47 76950 joined Derby Airways as G-AOGZ. It subsequently moved to France as F-OGDZ and in 1983 it is believed that the aircraft was converted into a Basler BT-67 turboprop aircraft for the Salvadorian Air Force, although other sources record the aircraft as remaining in use as a civil aircraft until being scrapped during the 1990s. (David Whitworth/Tony Clarke collection)

C-47 44-77084 served with the USAAF before joining the British civil register as G-AMZG. Pictured whilst operating with Transair, the aircraft is in the company's maintenance hangar at the long gone Croydon Airport during the early 1950s. (David Whitworth/Tony Clarke collection)

Proudly wearing the early post-war livery of British European Airways, C-47 G-AGJV went on to fly with British Midland before being sold to Antiguq as VP-LVM in 1980. (David Whitworth/Tony Clarke collection)

A classic moment of nostalgia from the late 1940s, with DC-3 VP-TBE pictured basking in the sun at Piarco Airport, Trinidad. (Eddie Coates collection)

Former C-353D 42-68774 was converted to DC-3A standard and issued to PAA as NC19116. It was sold to Cubana in 1949 and flew until 1961 when it was destroyed during the infamous Bay of Pigs invasion, after being strafed by counter-revolutionary B-26 Invaders. (Eddie Coates collection)

The Super DC-3 was designed by Douglas to offer greater capacity and performance. With an improved airframe and new engines, the aircraft had great potential but with surplus (and cheap) aircraft saturating the market, the design was not successful. Only five were delivered to Capital Airlines, but the US Navy embraced the derivative and ordered 100 conversions, which were designated as the R4D-8 and later the C-117D. (Eddie Coates collection)

Chapter 7

Commercial Success

Amerian Airlines accepted its first DST on April 29, 1936, although in order to save a significant amount of sales tax that would have been applicable in California, the aircraft was handed over in Phoenix, Arizona (as were subsequent aircraft). Passenger service began on June 26, when NC16001 named *Flagship New York* and NC16002 *Flagship Illinois* simultaneously departed from Newark and Chicago Airports. By the end of 1936, American Airlines had 20 aircraft in service while United had ten aircraft in operation. Orders from Eastern Airlines, TWA, PAA, KLM, Western Air Express and Swissair followed, and Douglas realized that it had a hugely successful aircraft, even though the company had not anticipated producing the aircraft in particularly large numbers. Initially, there had been some doubt as to whether production tooling would be required for more than 25 machines, but it was eventually decided to prepare for 50 aircraft. Nobody imagined that the same tooling would ultimately create 300 aircraft and that additional tooling, and three production plants would continue to produce the same aircraft in huge numbers. Despite having acquired the aircraft as a sleeper transport, American Airlines first used the DST as a standard daytime passenger aircraft, in which guise the aircraft was in effect a DC-3. It was not until September 18, 1936, that the airline embarked upon a coast-to-coast sleeper service, and the DST soon demonstrated an impressive westbound flight time of just 15 hours.

Restored to pristine condition, DC-3 NC28341 now proudly wears the post-war livery of Delta Air Lines. After having first served the company from 1940, the aircraft flew with a variety of operators until it was discovered in Puerto Rico during the early 1990s. Delta initiated an ambitious restoration program, and now the aircraft is maintained in flying condition, making appearances across the USA. (Delta Airlines)

Frank Azert recalls:

At the height of the DC-3's popularity, American Airlines owned 94 of these airplanes. At one time we flew them exclusively. When World War Two broke out, the US military drafted 47 of our aircraft. Fifteen of them were taken from our line fleet, the other 32 were modified to meet military specifications before they left the Douglas assembly line. These aircraft were variously designated as C-49Es, C-49Hs, C-50s and C-50As. Most C-49Es were fitted as ambulances. At least two of the H models served with the RAF. The 50s were sent to Australia and operated under civilian call signs. The 50As became 28-passenger troop carriers. As might be expected, some were casualties, others returned to AA after the war or went on to other roles and identities – some even winding up with competitors. American retired its last DC-3 in March of 1949.

Production of standard DC-3s for United Air Lines marked another milestone in the aircraft's history, primarily because the airline was part of the larger United Aircraft Technologies Company. As such, United clearly could not purchase the DC-3 with engines manufactured by a competing company (Wright), and this prompted the introduction of Pratt & Whitney Twin Wasp engines. Douglas did not have the engineering manpower to develop the new engine installation, and it was United's engineers that created all of the engineering drawings that were required. It cost the company additional money, but the result was a DST and DC-3 with an additional 14mph top speed and a better maximum altitude of 24,300ft.

C-47 G-AGZA joined Railway Air Services in 1945 and during December of the following year it crashed shortly after take-off from Northolt. The aircraft had been waiting in heavy snow for some time and its pilot was unable to gain height. Thankfully, there were no fatalities involved in this incident. (Tim McLelland collection)

Former USAAF 43-15333 joined Air France after World War Two, largely assigned to the company's Ringway—Le Bourget route. It was withdrawn and resold in 1968. (R. A. Scholefield collection)

Although technically designated as the DST, the DST was essentially the DC-3, tailored to the requirements of overnight passenger service. But Douglas developed the aircraft to fulfill both sleep and regular daytime services, and it was the "standard" DC-3 that soon became the aircraft that every airline wanted. The DST had a capacity for 28 passengers but with fore and aft-facing seats, this maximum figure was never actually used. The standard daytime passenger version (the DC-3) ultimately catered for 21 passengers, although it started out with a plan for 24. It could be converted to accommodate sleeper berths as required. However, for daytime passenger flying the aircraft needed additional cargo and baggage space and this necessitated a shift in the position of the baggage compartment bulkhead, which reduced the seating capacity to 21. This was still much better than the meagre capacity of just 14 that the DC-2 offered, and with operating costs that were only three percent higher than those of the DC-2, the commercial advantages of the DC-3 seemed clear. The DST soon fell from favor and only 38 aircraft were completed as DSTs, after which all new aircraft to emerge were DC-3s. The rather archaic VIP compartment inevitably suffered a similar fate with many airlines, and without this cabin section, passenger seating could be raised to 28. By 1939 some 350 DC-3s had been manufactured, and production showed no signs of slowing. License manufacture of the aircraft was agreed with Fokker, although the beginning of World War Two prevented the company from building any, and only 63 aircraft were distributed on behalf of Douglas. The Soviet Union acquired 21 DC-3s and a pair of unassembled airframes, designating home-produced aircraft as the PS-84, denoting the Passazhirskii Samolet Plant 84, located near Moscow. In 1942, the aircraft was renamed as the Li-2 in recognition of engineer Boris Lisunov, who had spent two years with Douglas, studying aircraft production. The DC-3's engines were replaced by the Shvetsov M-62, developed from the Wright engine fitted to the DC-2, creating a slight change in the shape of the aircraft's engine cowling that visually differentiates the Li-2 from its Western counterparts. Precise figures are difficult to determine, but some 3,500 DC-3s are known to have been manufactured in the USSR, although at least one Soviet official claimed that the figure may have been as high as 7,500. Rather ironically, despite never paying any license money to Douglas, the USSR also received more than 700 military variants of the DC-3 (the C-47) as part of America's Lend Lease arrangements. After World War Two, many of these aircraft became part of

DC-3 G-AHCY was the victim of a tragic accident on August 19, 1949. Due to errors in navigation and incorrect descent and approach procedures, the aircraft crashed into high ground at Saddleworth, en route to Ringway on a flight from Belfast. The crew and 21 passengers were killed in the tragedy. (*Aeroplane*)

Aeroflot's fleet, while others went to other Eastern Bloc airlines. Japan also embraced the DC-3, largely because of its rewarding experience with the DC-2. Dai Nippon operated a fleet of more than 20 aircraft prior to World War Two, and Mitsui (part of Nakajima) obtained production rights for the aircraft, although it was the Imperial Japanese Navy that was secretly behind the purchase, with dark plans to use the aircraft as part of a planned invasion of the East Indies. With military use firmly in mind, the Japanese-produced DC-3s were designated as the L2D2, with imported DC-3s designated as the L2D1.

Of course, history records that the DC-3 eventually became equally famous as both a commercial airliner and a military transport. The US Army purchased versions of the DC-2 that were successfully used as cargo aircraft, and it was inevitable that there would be great interest in the DST. When World War Two began to demand huge increases in American aircraft production, the DC-3 re-emerged as the legendary C-47 transport, and although this aircraft is the subject of a very different story, it is important to note that the C-47 eventually became a major part of the commercial aviation market after the war, when seemingly countless examples of the transporter became redundant, and the military C-47 effectively became the DC-3 in all but name. Surplus C-47s were readily available and cost very little, and this encouraged many small commercial operators to either enter into the air transport business, or rapidly develop their existing arrangements. The C-47 inevitably became known as the DC-3 (or "Dakota" in the United Kingdom), and when fitted with passenger seating, the C-47 was in essence a DC-3 with the addition of a large cargo door. In time, the DC-3 was overshadowed by its former military counterpart, simply because so many redundant C-47s had saturated a very eager market. Remarkably, the DC-3 and C-47 can still be seen all around the world, most aircraft having changed very little since the days when they were manufactured. Although the assertion that "the only replacement for a DC-3 is another DC-3" is undoubtedly a cliché, it is certainly true that the DC-3's rugged construction, good performance and economical operating costs still make the aircraft attractive to smaller commercial companies that require a "cheap and cheerful" transport. It's also fair to say that even Douglas could not really improve upon the DC-3, and even though bigger and more capable airliners gradually followed, there has never been another aircraft that can offer the same economy, ease of maintenance, good range, good capacity, ruggedness and reliability. Douglas tried to create a "Super DC-3" but with more power and more capacity, the Super DC-3 was also more expensive, and only a handful of these derivatives ever entered commercial service, even though the US military did at least show more enthusiasm in the design. In more recent years, there have been various projects to equip surviving DC-3s with turboprop engines, and these aircraft (most notably the Basler BT-67) are undoubtedly versatile, they still cannot beat the simplicity and (most importantly) inexpensiveness of the basic DC-3 airframe. It is almost impossible to establish precisely how many DC-3 and C-47 aircraft were ultimately produced, such was the aircraft's ubiquitous presence and enduring popularity. Douglas' records suggest that 10,632 were produced, although the complete figure is undoubtedly significantly higher and is probably closer to 18,000. The DC-3 eventually lost its place in widespread regular airline service as larger and more capable aircraft emerged, but the DC-3 endured, becoming the aircraft of choice for countless smaller commercial operators across the globe. Given the aircraft's supremely successful history, versatility, practicality and sheer durability, it seems to be more than likely that when the first flight of Donald Douglas' DC-1 is celebrated in 2033, there will still be more than a few DC-3s able to fly-by in salute.

DC-3 XC-CFE, operated by the Federal Commission for Electricity, and named *La Antorcha*, pictured during a visit to San Francisco in September 1960. (Tim McLelland collection)

Chapter 8

Specifications

GENERAL CHARACTERISTICS (DC-3A)

Crew: 2

Capacity: 21–32 passengers (27 standard)

or cargo combination

Length: 64ft 8in (19.7m)

Wingspan: 95ft 2in (29.0m)

Height: (Top of fin) 16ft 11in (5.16m)

Wing area: 987sq ft (91.7 m^2)

Empty weight: 16,865lb (7,650kg)

Gross weight: 25,199lb (11,430kg)

Fuel capacity: 822 gal. (3736 liters)

Powerplant: 2 × Wright R-1820 Cyclone 9-cyl. air-cooled radial piston engine, 1,100hp (820kW) each

Powerplant: 2 × Pratt & Whitney R-1830-S1C3G Twin Wasp 14-cyl. air-cooled two row radial piston engine, 1,200hp (890kW) each

Propellers: 3-bladed Hamilton Standard 23E50 series, 11.5ft (3.5m) diameter

Maximum speed: 200kn; 370km/h (230mph) at 8,500ft (2,590m)

Cruise speed: 180kn; 333km/h (207 mph)

Stall speed: 58.2kn (67mph; 108km/h)

Service ceiling: 23,200ft (7,100m)

Rate of climb: 1,130ft/min (5.7m/s)

Wing loading: 25.5lb/sq ft (125kg/m^2)

Power/mass: 0.0952hp/lb (156.5w/kg)

Cargo Load: 7,000Ibs

Fuel Burn: 90 imp gal/hr

Resplendent in high-visibility orange trim, part of Swissair's DC-3 Training School fleet is pictured in 1968 at Zurich Airport.

G-AMWW was one of four DC-3s (C-47s) operated by Skyways of London, a large British operator of non-scheduled European services post-war. The company ended operations in 1962, only to re-emerge in 1975 for a further five years, after which financial difficulties led to the demise of this once-famous operator. (*Aeroplane*)

COMMERCIAL VARIANTS

DST: The Douglas Sleeper Transport. The DC-3 initial variant, accommodating 24 passengers during day flights and fitted out with 16 sleeper berths in the main cabin for night flights.

DC-3: The main production variant, normally fitted with 21 passenger seats.

DC-3A: Improved version of the basic DC-3, redesigned with two 1,200hp (894.84kW) Pratt & Whitney R-1830-21 radial piston engines. Designation also applied to some former C-47 aircraft converted to civil use.

DC-3B: A further improved DC-3 powered by two 1,100hp (820.27kW) Wright R-1820-G101 Cyclone, or two 1,200hp (894.84 kW) Wright R-1820-G202A Cyclone engines.

DC-3C: This designation was applied to former military C-47, C-53 and R4D aircraft that were built by Douglas Aircraft in 1946 and resold to the civil market.

DC-3D: Additional designation for 28 new aircraft built by Douglas in 1946 for civil airline operations, using components transferred from uncompleted United States Army Air Force (USAAF) C-117s.

DC-3S: The Super DC-3. Design based on the basic DC-3 but with a new wing and tail layout. Powered by two 1,450hp (1,081.26kW) Pratt & Whitney R-2000-D7, or 1,475hp (1,099.91kW) Wright R-1820-C9HE Cyclone engines. Aircraft were converted by Douglas between 1949 and 1950 from existing DC-3 and R4D airframes.

Lisunov PS-84: Derived from the DC-3, a 14–28 seat passenger airliner developed in the USSR (a copy of the DC-3) powered by two 900hp (671.13kW) Shvetsov M-62/1,000hp (745.70kW) Shvetsov ASh-62 engines. Featuring a slightly smaller wingspan and a higher empty weight, it was fitted with lower-powered engines as compared to the DC-3. The standard cargo door was transposed to the starboard side of the fuselage.

Designations for commercial variants assigned to military use
C-41A: Only one DC-3A (40-070) was modified into a VIP transport, powered by two 1,200 hp (895 kW) Pratt & Whitney R-1830-21 radial piston engines, and used as a transport for the US secretary of war. The Douglas C-41 was not a DC-3 derivative but a modification of a Douglas C-33.

C-48: One aircraft, formerly with United Air Lines as a DC-3A, impressed into military service.

C-48A: Three DC-3As with 18-seat interiors transferred to military use.

C-48B: Sixteen former United Air Lines DST-As with 16-berth interiors used in the United States as air ambulances.

C-48C: Sixteen DC-3As with 21-seat interiors, assigned to military use.

C-49: DC-3 and DST models, some 138 impressed into service as C-49, C-49A, C-49B, C-49C, C-49D, C-49E, C-49F, C-49G, C-49H, C-49J, and C-49K aircraft.

C-50: Various DC-3 models, 14 assigned to military use as the C-50, C-50A, C-50B, C-50C and C-50D.

C-51: One aircraft ordered by Canadian Colonial Airlines impressed into US service, featuring a starboard-side door.

C-52: DC-3A aircraft with R-1830 engines, a batch of five transferred to military service as C-52, C-52A, C-52B, C-52C and C-52D.

C-68: Two DC-3As with 21-seat interiors, transferred to military use.

C-84: One DC-3B aircraft, reassigned to the US Military.

R4D-2: Two Eastern Air Lines DC-3s transferred to US Navy service as VIP transports, subsequently designated as R4D-2F and later as the R4D-2Z.

R4D-4: Ten DC-3s, reassigned to military use.

R4D-4R: Seven DC-3s refitted as military staff transports.

R4D-4Q: Radar countermeasures version of the R4D-4.

Dakota II: Royal Air Force designation for DC-3s, transferred to the RAF.

Military production
C-47 Skytrain: The basic military version of the DC-3A with seats for 27 troops. Some 965 manufactured, including 12 to the United States Navy (USN), designated as the R4D-1.

C-47A: C-47 with a 24-volt electrical system. Some 5,254 manufactured, including USN aircraft that were designated as the R4D-5.

RC-47A: C-47A equipped for photographic reconnaissance and Electronic Intelligence (ELINT) duties.

SC-47A: C-47A equipped for Search Air Rescue. Redesignated HC-47A in 1962.

VC-47A: C-47A equipped for the VIP transport role.

C-47B: Powered by R-1830-90 engines with superchargers and extra fuel capacity to fly China–Burma–India routes. Some 3,364 manufactured.

VC-47B: C-47B equipped for the VIP transport role.

XC-47C: C-47 tested with Edo Model 78 floats for potential use as a seaplane.

C-47D: C-47B with superchargers that were removed after World War Two.

AC-47D: Gunship aircraft fitted with three 0.30in (7.62mm) machine guns, firing through side windows.

EC-47D: C-47D with equipment for the Airborne Early Warning role. Prior to 1962, this aircraft was designated as the AC-47D.

NC-47D: C-47D modified for test and evaluation duties.

RC-47D: C-47D equipped for photographic reconnaissance and ELINT operations.

SC-47D: C-47D equipped for Search Air Rescue. Redesignated as the HC-47D in 1962.

VC-47D: C-47D equipped for the VIP transport role.

C-47E: A modified cargo variant with accommodation for 27–28 passengers or 18–24 litters.

C-47F: YC-129 redesignated as the Super DC-3 prototype for evaluation by the United States Air Force (USAF). Subsequently transferred to the US Navy as an XR4D-8.

C-47L/M: C-47H/J equipped for the support of American Legation United States Naval Attaché (ALUSNA) and Military Assistance Advisory Group (MAAG) missions.

EC-47N/P/Q: C-47A and 'D' variants, modified for ELINT operations. The 'N' and 'P' versions differed in coverage of radio bands, while the 'Q' carried digital equipment, replacing analogue equipment fitted in the 'N' and 'P', and featured redesigned antenna equipment plus uprated engines.

C-47R: One C-47M modified for high altitude work, specifically for missions in Ecuador.

C-53 Skytrooper: Troop transport version of the C-47.

XC-53A Skytrooper: One aircraft manufactured with full-span slotted flaps and hot-air leading edge deicing systems.

C-53B Skytrooper: Winter operations version of C-53 with extra fuel capacity and a separate navigator's station. One batch of eight manufactured.

C-53C Skytrooper: The C-53 with a larger door fitted to the port side of the fuselage. Seventeen aircraft built.

C-53D Skytrooper: The C-53C with a new 24V DC electrical system; 159 manufactured.

C-117A Skytrooper: The C-47B with 24-seats in an airline-style interior for staff transport use. Sixteen built.

VC-117A: Three C-117s operated in the VIP transport role.

SC-117A: One C-117C converted for air-sea rescue duties.

C-117B/VC-117B: One aircraft manufactured with high-altitude superchargers removed. Further conversions from C-117As completed as the later VC-117B.

C-117D: R4D-8 redesignated by the USN and Marine Corps.

LC-117D: R4D-8L redesignated by the USN and Marine Corps.

TC-117D: R4D-8T redesignated by the USN and Marine Corps.

VC-117D: R4D-8Z redesignated by the USN and Marine Corps.

YC-129: Super DC-3 prototype. Evaluated by the USAF and redesignated as the C-47F and subsequently transferred to the USN as the XR4D-8.

CC-129: Canadian Armed Forces designation applied to the C-47 from 1970 onwards.

XCG-17: One C-47 airframe tested as a 40-seat troop glider with engines removed and faired over.

R4D: General designation applied to US Navy and Marine Corps aircraft, including production airframes, impressed civil aircraft and aircraft transferred from the USAAF/USAF.

R4D-1 Skytrain: The USN/Marine Corps version of the C-47.

R4D-3: Batch of 20 C-53Cs transferred to the USN.

R4D-5: C-47A variant with a 24-volt electrical system, replacing the 12-volt system of the C-47. Redesignated as the C-47H in 1962, 238 transferred from USAF.

R4D-5L: The R4D-5 designed for use in Antarctica. Redesignated as the LC-47H in 1962.

R4D-5Q: The R4D-5 designed for use as special Electronic Countermeasures trainer. Redesignated as the EC-47H in 1962.

R4D-5R: The R4D-5 designed for use as a personnel transport for 21 passengers, or as a trainer aircraft. Redesignated as the TC-47H in 1962.

R4D-5S: The R4D-5 designed use as a special Anti-Submarine Warfare trainer. Redesignated as the SC-47H in 1962.

R4D-5Z:
The R4D-5 modified for use as a VIP transport. Redesignated as the VC-47H in 1962.

R4D-6: Applied to 157 C-47Bs transferred to the USN. Redesignated as the C-47J in 1962.

R4D-6L, Q, R, S, and Z: Applied to variants in the same way as the R4D-5 series. Redesignated as the LC-47J, EC-47J, TC-47J, SC-47J, and VC-47J, respectively, in 1962.

R4D-7: Some 44 TC-47Bs transferred from the USAF for use as navigational trainers. Redesignated as the TC-47K in 1962.

R4D-8: Applied to R4D-5 and R4D-6 aircraft fitted with modified wings and redesigned tail surfaces. Redesignated as the C-117D in 1962.

R4D-8L: Applied to R4D-8 aircraft converted for Antarctic use. Redesignated as the LC-117D in 1962.

R4D-8T: Applied to R4D-8 aircraft converted into crew trainers. Redesignated as the TC-117D in 1962.

R4D-8Z: Applied to R4D-8 aircraft converted into staff transports. Redesignated as the VC-117D in 1962.

Dakota I: RAF designation for the C-47 and R4D-1.

Dakota III: RAF designation for the C-47A.

Dakota IV: RAF designation for the C-47B.

Li-2: Some 4,937 aircraft manufactured, derived from the DC-3 as a military transport aircraft with defensive armament. License-built in the USSR, the designation came into use from September 1942.

Li-2D: Paratroop transport version of the Li-2 transport with reinforced floor and tie-downs, together with a cargo door (of different design to the DC-3) on the port side of the fuselage.

Li-2P: Commercial passenger transport variant.

Li-2PG: Commercial combined passenger and cargo version.

Li-2R: Reconnaissance and intelligence-gathering version, with additional windows fitted behind the cockpit.

Li-2VV: Bomber version.

Li-2V: High-altitude weather surveillance version of the Li-2, equipped with turbocharged engines.

Li-3: Yugoslavian version, equipped with American Pratt & Whitney R-1830 engines.

Li-2T: Polish variant, designed for bomber crew training.

L2D: Some 487 aircraft, license-built in Japan for the Imperial Japanese Naval Air Service (IJNAS).

LXD1: A single DC-3 supplied for evaluation by the IJNAS.

L2D2: Personnel transport variant fitted with Mitsubishi Kinsei 43 radials engines.

L2D2-1: Cargo carrying version incorporating an enlarged cargo door.

L2D3 and L2D3-1: Modified versions fitted with two Mitsubishi Kinsei 51 engines, each rated at 1,325hp (975kW).

L2D3a and L2D3-1a: Production standard variant fitted with two Mitsubishi Kinsei 53 engines, each rated at 1,325hp (975kW).

L2D4 and L2D4-1: Military armed version, fitted with a 13mm machine gun inside a dorsal turret, together with two 7.7mm machine guns inside the left and right fuselage hatches.

L2D5: Remanufactured variant with wooden components replacing steel structures. Powered by two Mitsubishi Kinsei 62 engines, each rated at 1,590hp (1,170kW).

CONVERSIONS

Various DC-3 aircraft were modified to carry new engines, acting as test beds in support of engine development programs. The Rolls-Royce Dart, Armstrong Siddeley Mamba and the Pratt & Whitney Canada PT6A turbines were all tested on DC-3 aircraft.

Dart Dakota: Acquired from Field Aircraft Services Ltd in 1950 with engine installations paid for by the Ministry of Supply, two aircraft were flown as G-AMDB and G-ALXN forming the "Dart Development Unit" and used to develop operating procedures in advance of the introduction of the Vickers Viscount with British European Airways. A single C-47 (G-AMDB c/n 14987/26432) was also converted and subsequently restored to DC-3 standard after trials and route-proving, rejoining BEA as a standard DC-3 until it was sold in 1962. A further C-47B-1-DK (c/n 25613 and 43-48352/KJ829) was also converted for use by Rolls-Royce for trials of the 1,540hp (1,148.38kW) Rolls-Royce Dart. This aircraft (given the test registration G-37-2) flew with two Dart engines. Ultimately, it was sold to Tyne Tees Airways in April 1963 and scrapped in 1965.

Mamba Dakota: A single C-47 (KJ839) was converted to carry 1,475hp (1,099.91kW) Armstrong Siddeley Mamba turboprop engines, for in-flight trials. DC-3/2000 designation applied to DC-3 engine conversions performed by Airtech, Canada, beginning in 1987. Powered by two PZL ASz-62IT radials.

Basler BT-67: Applied to a major DC-3 conversion, comprising of a stretched fuselage, strengthened structure and modern avionics. Powered by two Pratt & Whitney Canada PT-6A-67R turboprop engines.

Conroy Turbo Three: One DC-3 was converted by Conroy Aircraft to carry two Rolls-Royce Dart Mk 510 turboprop engines.

Conroy Super-Turbo-Three: One aircraft converted by Conroy Aircraft to carry two Rolls-Royce Dart Mk.510 turboprop engines, the airframe having been converted from a Super DC-3.

Conroy Tri-Turbo-Three: One DC-3 converted by Conroy Aircraft to carry three Pratt & Whitney Canada PT-6A turboprops.

USAC DC-3 Turbo Express: Turboprop conversion created by the United States Aircraft Corporation. Featuring Pratt & Whitney Canada PT6A-45R turboprop engines with an extended forward fuselage to maintain the aircraft's center of gravity.

C-47T: Designation applied to aircraft modified to a Basler BT-67 standard.

BSAS C-47-65ARTP Turbo Dakota: Conversion comprising of two Pratt & Whitney Canada PT6A-65R engines and a stretched fuselage, designed for the South African Air Force (SAAF).

BSAS C-47-67RTP Turbo Dakota: Conversion comprising of two Pratt & Whitney Canada PT6A-67R engines and a stretched fuselage, designed for the SAAF.

BSAS C-47-67FTP Turbo Dakota: Conversion comprising of two Pratt & Whitney Canada PT6A-67F engines and a stretched fuselage, designed for the SAAF.

A British European Airways C-47 pictured on a stormy day during the early 1950s in front of the majestic terminal at Liverpool's Speke Airport. (*Aeroplane*)

A wide-angle view of the C-47's flight deck, this aircraft being G-AMRA, operated by Air Atlantique. This aircraft is expected to resume pleasure flying operations from Newquay Airport/RAF St. Mawgan, where the company's Classic Air Force is now located. (Air Atlantique)

Only one flying example of the license-built Lisunow Li-2 has survived outside of North Korea, this being Hungarian-registered HA-LIX, which operates sight-seeing flights and also makes regular air show appearances. (Julian Herzog)

G-AMPO was a former RAF C-47 that saw regular service with a variety of British operators post-World War Two. Pictured in the livery of Starways, the aircraft also flew with operators such as Eastern Airways and Air Atlantique before being withdrawn from use at Coventry. More recently the aircraft has been placed on static display in RAF markings at RAF Lyneham, although the closure of that base now places the aircraft's long-term future in doubt. (Barry Friend)

Resplendent in the markings of Ozark Airlines, this DC-3 illustrates the retractable landing gear doors and fairings that were introduced by Douglas as a means of improving the DC-3s performance. The modification proved to be of little value and only a few DC-3s were flown with the modifications fitted. (Eddie Coates collection)

Although this DC-3 was displayed at Boeing's Museum of Flight as NC91008, this aircraft was in fact NC15748.

Possibly the ultimate expression of the original Douglas DC-3 design is the Basler BT-67, incorporating an improved airframe and Pratt & Whitney turboprop engines. Numerous DC-3/C-47 aircraft have been refurbished and converted by Basler and aircraft continue to be produced in response to orders from companies requiring inexpensive, versatile aircraft for specialized work. A significant number of these conversions also operate in military service. (Basler Turbo Conversions)

Basler BT-67 modifications overview diagram, illustrating the main changes to the basic DC-3 airframe. (Basler Turbo Conversions)

BASLER BT-67
STANDARD CONVERSION

Fuselage Stretch

Improved Hydraulic System

Improved Fuel System
800 Gallon Capacity

All New Cockpit

Structural Reinforcement

Composite Nacelle

Expander Tube Brakes

Improved Wing Tip and Leading Edge

New - Part 25 Electrical System

Original

BT-67 Conversion

5 Blade Metal Propeller Pratt & Whitney (PT6A-67R) Turbine Engine

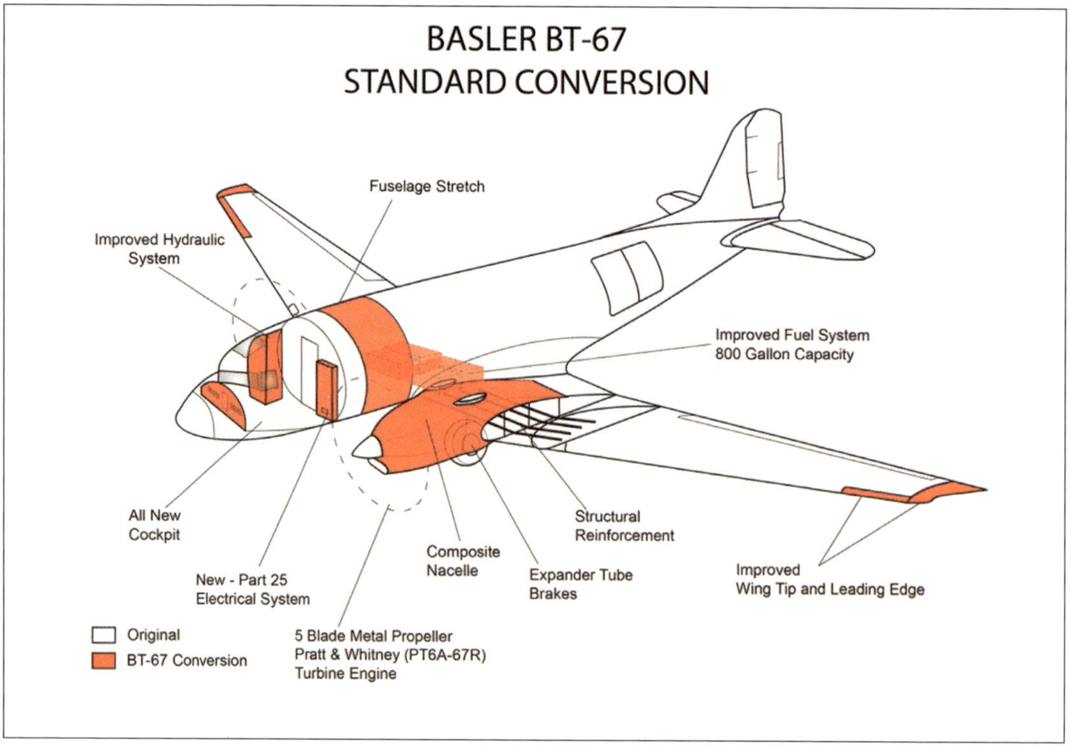

To commemorate the centennial of the Wright Brother's flight at Kitty Hawk, US charity Portraits of Hope worked with Nasa to invite thousands of seriously ill children to create a colorful design for one of the 100 historical planes to be featured at the ceremonies. One such recipient of these paint schemes was DC-3 N143D, seen here over the historic Kitty Hawk coastline. (Photo via NASA)

DC-3 F-BEIG seen at the 1967 Paris Air Show at Le Bourget. The aircraft was assigned to Air France's Training School but leased to Normandie Air Services. (*Aeroplane*)